T0074560

Statistical Trend Analysis of Physically Unclonable Functions

Statistical Trend Analysis of Physically Unclonable Functions

An Approach via Text Mining

Behrouz Zolfaghari
Khodakhast Bibak
Takeshi Koshiba
Hamid R. Nemati
Pinaki Mitra

CRC Press
Taylor & Francis Group
Boca Raton London New York

CRC Press is an imprint of the
Taylor & Francis Group, an **informa** business

First edition published 2021
by CRC Press
6000 Broken Sound Parkway NW, Suite 300, Boca Raton, FL 33487-2742

and by CRC Press
2 Park Square, Milton Park, Abingdon, Oxon, OX14 4RN

CRC Press is an imprint of Taylor & Francis Group, LLC

Library of Congress Cataloging-in-Publication Data

ISBN: 978-0-367-75455-6 (hbk)
ISBN: 978-1-003-16710-5 (ebk)

Typeset in Latin Modern font
by KnowledgeWorks Global Ltd.

Contents

Book Description

Physically unclonable functions (PUFs) translate unavoidable variations in certain parameters of materials, waves or devices into random and unique signals. They have found many applications in the Internet of things (IoT), authentication systems, FPGA industry, several other areas in communications and related technologies, and many commercial products.

In this book, we first present a review on cryptographic hardware and hardware-assisted cryptography. The review highlights PUF as a mega trend in research on cryptographic hardware design. Afterwards, we present a combined survey and research work on PUFs using a systematic approach. As part of the survey aspect, we present a state-of-the-art analysis as well as a taxonomy on PUFs, derive a life cycle and establish an ecosystem for the technology. In another part of the survey, we study the evolutionary history of PUFs, and suggest strategies for further research in this area.

In the research side, this book presents a novel approach for trend analysis that can be applied to any technology or research area (in fact, the trend analysis on PUFs is presented just as a case study). In this method, we first use a text-mining tool that extracts 1020 keywords from the titles of the sample papers. Then, a classifying tool classifies the keywords into 295 meaningful research topics. The popularity of each topic is then numerically measured and analyzed over the course of time through a statistical analysis on the number of research papers related to the topic as well as the number of their citations. We try to identify the most popular topics in four different domains: over the history of PUFs, during the recent years, in top conferences and in top journals. The results are used to present an evolution study as well as a trend analysis and develop a roadmap for future research in this area. This method gives an automatic popularity-based statistical trend analysis, which eliminates the need for passing personal judgments about the direction of trends, and provides concrete evidence to the future direction of research on PUFs. Another advantage of this method is the possibility of studying a whole lot of existing research works (more than 700 in this book). Furthermore, our approach makes it possible to depend more on informative figures, tables and charts instead of text while reporting our results.

Keywords: Physically Unclonable Function, Text Mining, Trend Analysis, Evolution Study, Future Roadmap, Statistics, Hardware-Assisted Cryptography, Cryptographic Hardware.

About the Authors

Behrouz Zolfaghari is currently a postdoctoral fellow at Indian Institute of Technology Guwahati. His research interests include hardware-oriented cryptography, information-theoretic cryptography, information theory, VLSI design and discrete mathematics.

Khodakhast Bibak is an Assistant Professor at the Department of Computer Science and Software Engineering at Miami University. Previously, he was a Postdoctoral Research Associate (September 2017 - August 2018) in the Coordinated Science Laboratory at the University of Illinois at Urbana-Champaign. Before this, Khodakhast was a Postdoctoral Research Fellow (May-August 2017) at the Department of Computer Science, University of Victoria, from where he also received his PhD (April 2017). He earned a Master of Mathematics degree (April 2013) at the Department of Combinatorics and Optimization, University of Waterloo, where he was also a member of the Centre for Applied Cryptographic Research (CACR). Khodakhast's research interests are Cybersecurity, Applied Cryptography, Information Theory, Communications, Quantum Information Science (QIS), and related areas.

Takeshi Koshiba received the PhD degree from Tokyo Institute of Technology. He is a full professor at the Department of Mathematics, the Faculty of Education and Integrated Arts and Sciences, Waseda University, Japan. His interests include theoretical and applied cryptography, the randomness in algorithms, and quantum computing and cryptography.

Hamid R. Nemati is a full Professor of Information Systems at the University of North Carolina at Greensboro. He received his PhD from the University of Georgia in Information Technology and Management Science and his MBA from The University of Massachusetts. He is internationally recognized for his research in various aspects of Information Technology, including data analytics, big data, information security and privacy, organizational and behavioral aspects of Information Technology development and use. He has extensive professional experience as a developer, an analyst and project leader and has been a consultant for numerous major corporations. He has published nine books and over 120 peer reviewed academic publications in various premier scholarly and professional journals and conference proceedings

Pinaki Mitra is currently an associate professor at Department of Computer Science & Engineering, IIT Guwahati. He obtained his B. Tech in Computer Science and Engineering from Jadavpur University, Kolkata in 1987, India and his M. Tech in Computer Science and Engineering from Indian Institute of Science Bangalore, India in 1989. Finally, he obtained his Ph. D from Simon Fraser University, Canada in 1994. He worked on a project at Jadavpur University, department of Computer Science and Engineering. Subsequently he joined National Institute of Management, Kolkata, and served as an assistant professor. He joined IIT Guwahati in December, 2004. His research interest includes Cryptography, Network Security, Computer Graphics, Multimedia and Machine Learning.

CHAPTER 1

Introduction

Unique and random signals or bit sequences play important roles in security-related applications. Unique bit sequences are used in applications such as device/user authentication, and randomness is used for key generation, obfuscation and similar purposes. In recent years, it has been shown that some unclonable properties in some elements such as devices, waves or materials can vary randomly in different experiments or uniquely between similar elements. PUFs use these properties to create random [315] and/or unique [120] signals. Different aspects of PUFs have been of interest to researchers in recent years [124] [339] [109]. The architecture of a PUF is shown in the left side of Figure 1.1. The right side shows the icon by which we represent a PUF in this book.

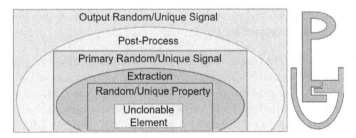

Figure 1.1 PUF Architecture.

As shown in Figure 1.1, the core of a PUF is an unclonable element, to which we simply refer as the element for short. The element can be a material such as paper [371], carbon nanotube [181], silicon [69], germanium [349], phosphor [151], photonic crystal

[214], metal [362] and organic semiconductor [283]. It can even be a wave such as optical [143] or magnetic [228] wave. But most commonly, it is a device. It varies from sensors [50]; electrical devices such as voltage dividers [356] and solar cells [183]; micro-electronic devices such as diodes [281], transistors [380] and memristors [53]; logic gates such as NAND [193] and XOR [209]; and memories such as SRAM [112] and DRAM [338]; to processors [383], microprocessors [198] and microcontrollers [381]. It can be seen in Figure 1.1

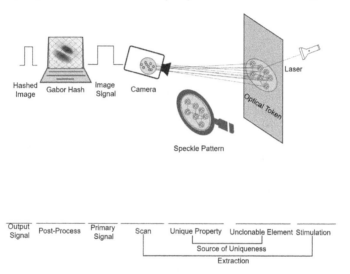

Figure 1.2 The Architecture of an Optical PUF and the Match with the Architecture in Figure 1.1.

that the element along with its unique/random property (property for short) builds the source of uniqueness/randomness (source for short). The property varies from eye-opening oscillation [131], biological parameters [361] and spin transfer characteristics [228] to geometry [76] and breakdown positions [64], leakage [194] and resistance [93], decay [316] or aging effect [233], write time [379], switching time [337] and write contention written value [205].

The extraction process generates the primary unique/random signal from the source. This process is usually performed by a stimulation mechanism, which activates the unique/random property, and a scan mechanism, which quantizes the property. This process is usually realized using a circuit, which we call the extraction circuit. The extraction circuit can vary from arbiters [44] and multiplexers [140] to ring oscillators [186] and pseudo-linear feedback shift registers (Pseudo-LFSRs) [263]. The primary signal often lacks the required level of properties such as randomness including entropy [317], non-linearity [17], chaos [243] and bit aliasing [257], stability [392] and quality [56]. Therefore, it needs some post-process such as bit selection [372], entropy distillation [384], helper data algorithm [219], error correction [69] or random substitution/permutation [133].

Figure 1.1 suggests the model given in equation 1.1 for a PUF.

$$\mathcal{S}_{out} = \Pi_{post}(\mathcal{S}_{pr}), \text{ where } \mathcal{S}_{pr} = \Gamma_{\tau,\sigma}(\varepsilon, \upsilon) \tag{1.1}$$

In equation 1.1, ε and υ represent the unclonable element and the unique property, respectively. In this equation, τ and σ denote the stimulation and the scan process, respectively. Moreover, $\Gamma_{\tau,\sigma}$, $\mathcal{S}_{pr}$, Π_{post} and $\mathcal{S}_{out}$ represent the extraction process, the primary signal, the post-process and the output signal, respectively. In applications that require random number generation, a sequence of stimulations τ_i are applied, and the resulting output signal $\mathcal{S}_{out}$ plays the role of the random signal. In authentication-based applications, a set of $(\tau, \mathcal{S}_{out})$ couples (challenge-response pairs) are assigned to each (ε, υ) couple (source of randomness). This assignment can be modeled by equation 1.2.

$$(\tau, \mathcal{S}_{out}) = \rho(\varepsilon, \upsilon) \tag{1.2}$$

The relation ρ is usually stored in a database. In this case, authentication is accomplished by applying a set of challenges τ and comparing the resulting responses $\mathcal{S}_{out}$ against the ones stored in the database.

As an example, for the general architecture shown in Figure 1.1, we can mention the optical PUF initially introduced in [270] and [271]. The architecture of this PUF is shown in Figure 1.2.

In the optical PUF shown in Figure 1.2, the unique element is an optical token. In the token, a number of glass spheres capable of refracting light beams are mixed on a transparent epoxy plate. Different sources and directions of refraction cause this element to generate a very irregular wavefront when radiated with a laser. This irregular emerging wavefront creates a unique speckle pattern, which plays the role of the unique property. The extraction mechanism consists of a CCD camera that records the speckle pattern in the form of a digital primary signal. Finally, the post-process is a Gabor hash, which creates the output image signal.

Not surprisingly, the diversity explained above opens a broad spectrum of PUF-related research areas in front of researchers. This has led to a huge number of research projects, which highlight PUF as a popular research topic. In this book, we measure the popularity of a research topic by the number of published research reports related to the topic and the number of citations to the reports. Figure 1.3 shows the popularity of PUF as a research topic over the course of time.

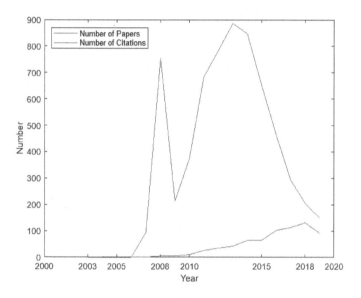

Figure 1.3 Number of Papers and Citations.

The large number of publications and citations shows the popularity of PUFs. The gap between the two curves in Figure 1.3 indicates the large average number of citations to research works published in this area. But the following point needs to be noted in this regard. As seen in Figure 1.3, the number of citations for PUF-related studies has declined after a peak in 2015. This trend may be rationalized as researchers needing time to use recent results. But the number of papers is declining as well after a peak in 2018, which can be considered a sign of saturation.

A proper trend analysis or future roadmap can help researchers identify new and unsaturated aspects of PUFs to work on. While there are several reviews in this area, some of them are outdated, and some do not present a trend analysis or a future roadmap. In addition, there are some more important shortcomings in the existing reviews, surveys and trend analyses. First, they have not reviewed a large-enough sample space, which leads to undependable trend identifications. Second, they have not taken a systematic statistical approach to evolution study, trend analysis or future roadmap development.

In this book, we present a systematic statistical trend analysis and evolution study on PUFs as well as a roadmap for future research in this area. Our statistical analysis is based on a sample space containing 693 published PUF-related research reports. An automatic text mining tool makes it possible to collect information from such a large sample space to be fed into the statistical analysis engine. The text mining tool is first trained by 577 random reports and then operates on the entire 693-report sample space. The text mining tool suggests 1020 keywords extracted from the reports, which are classified later into 295 meaningful research topics related to PUFs. The popularity of each individual topic is measured, and the topics are ranked on the basis of their popularity in the course of time, in recent years and in top journals and conferences. This ranking leads to the selection of some top topics, which help us study the evolution of PUFs, analyze the related trends and develop a future roadmap.

The following points need to be clarified regarding our approach, our methodology and the related working space.

1. Our sample space (consisting of research reports) has been selected in a way that guarantees the maximum level of dependability. The sample space is large enough, and the reports have been collected using an unbiased search with general keywords such as "PUF" and "Physically Unclonable Function". The search has been accomplished using the most common search engines such as Google and scientific databases, such as IEEExplore. Of course, there might be rare reports that do not implicitly mention such keywords in their titles despite their valuable relevant work [153]. But it is obvious that they cannot affect our statistical trend analysis.

2. For reports that contain keywords from more than one topic in their titles, the report and its citations are taken into account while analyzing the popularity of each topic. This approach does not affect our statistical results as we work only

with the total/average number of research works and citations, not correlations.

The novel aspects of this research can be explained as follows.

1. To the best of our knowledge, this is the first statistical trend analysis on PUFs. The number of papers and the number of citations are being used for the first time as statistical measures for popularity of PUF-related research topics. This is the first time these measures are being statistically analyzed in domains such as the entire history, recent years, top conferences and top journals

2. This is the first review wherein the topics are extracted by an automatic tool and especially using a text mining tools. Moreover, a corpus is presented in this book for text mining in PUF-related research reports, which is the first in its kind. Further, such a large number of topics are analyzed.

The rest of this book is organized as follows. Chapter 2 presents a systematic review on cryptographic hardware, hardware-assisted cryptography and related concepts. This chapter highlights PUF as a research trend in hardware-assisted cryptography. Chapter 3 presents a brief background study including the historical background of PUFs as well as how they have received focus from the industry, education programs and publishers. Chapter 4 presents preliminary discussions. This chapter first presents a review on existing surveys, and highlights their shortcomings. Then our motivations for the work of this book are discussed. In the next step, this chapter explains our trend analysis methodology and the related working space. The working space consists of the research reports used for training the text mining tool and the ones used by the statistical analysis. Chapter 5 introduces the corpora used by the text mining tool. Each topic in the corpora is individually analyzed from popularity point of view. Chapter 6 presents the trend analysis. In this chapter, first the most popular topics are highlighted. Then the evolution of PUFs is studied, and the trends are examined. Chapter 7 outlines topics for future research on PUF.

Note that the reports that have been used only by the text mining tool are included in the e-resource.

CHAPTER 2

Cryptographic Hardware and Hardware-Assisted Cryptography

Most cryptographic algorithms are computation-intensive. Thus, they need to be implemented in hardware in order to meet performance requirements of high-speed environments. Hardware implementation of cryptographic schemes has received a research focus since past decades due to higher performance compared with software implementation [262] [154]. Researchers have been interested in hardware implementation of many well-known cryptosystems such as AES [253], RSA [287] and Serpent [73]. Furthermore, different types of cryptographic hardware have been used in a variety of cryptography-related areas such as visual cryptography [149] and multiparty authentication [24]. Moreover, cryptographic hardware components have been used in several other applications, platforms and environments. To mention a few, one may refer to IoT [212] and IoT-based applications [340], biomedical applications [49], multimedia applications [294], ubiquitous computing [104], WSNs (wireless sensor networks) [138], RFID tags [13] and instant messaging [293].

A comprehensive, up-to-date survey on hardware-oriented cryptography and cryptographic hardware can pave the way for further research in this area, especially if it presents a trend analysis, and establishes a future roadmap. Although there are some surveys in this area, none of them comes with all the needed features. In this chapter, we try to review existing research reports on all the aspects of cryptographic hardware including their design, implementation, evaluation, classifications and applications. We analyze the existing research trends in this area. Our analyses highlight the role of PUF as a popular trend in recent research on hardware-oriented cryptography, which motivates our work in the next chapters. Moreover, we suggest outlines for further research on cryptographic hardware and related areas.

2.1   EXISTING SURVEYS

The literature in the area of hardware-oriented cryptography comes with some reviews and surveys, but the following shortcomings can be seen in these reports.

- Some existing surveys are too outdated for such a fast-moving area [28] [92].

- Some reports limit themselves to study a certain class of cryptographic hardware such as cryptographic processors [28].

- Some reviews focus on implementations based on specific hardware platforms such as FPGAs [180].

- Some focus on the hardware implementation of a specific type of cryptographic schemes such as symmetric-key cryptosystems [46], lattice-based cryptosystems [254] or elliptic-curve cryptography (ECC) [77].

- Others study hardware implementation of a certain cryptosystem such as IDEA [245].

- Some surveys focus on specific applications such as data outsourcing [325] or applications in specific environments such as IoT [23], resource-constrained devices [180] or bus encryption [92].

- Some reviews focus on a specific aspect of hardware-oriented cryptography such as the evaluation of cryptographic hardware [137].

The above shortcomings motivate our work in this chapter. In the following, we briefly study some existing surveys and reviews in a chronological order.

A review on the applications of cryptographic processors has been presented in [28] along with a classification of attacks on these devices as well as countermeasures. The authors of [92] have reviewed existing hardware solutions for encrypting the data and instructions exchanged between the CPU and external memories installed in ubiquitous embedded devices connected through USB buses. Existing solutions (at the time of publications) for symmetric and asymmetric cryptography in embedded hardware have been reviewed in [91]. The authors review recent developments in this area for symmetric and asymmetric ciphers, targeting embedded hardware and software.

Techniques for high-performance hardware implementation of ECC have been studied and classified in [77] with a focus on reconfigurable scalar multipliers. The authors of [77] have presented a roadmap for future research on this topic. Different hardware implementations of the IDEA cipher using ASIC and FPGA have been discussed in [245] along with the considered design objectives such as throughput and area. The authors of [46] have argued that most hardware implementations of cryptosystems have sacrificed key management security to achieve higher performance and/or flexibility. They studied the minority of related research works that tackle this problem via proposing solutions based on multiple cryptographic processors and reconfigurable cryptographic arrays. A brief review on cryptographic co-processors has been presented in [119]. The authors of [119] have highlighted some challenges faced by designers of cryptographic co-processors.

Lightweight symmetric ciphers, which are used in devices with power and area limitations, have been reviewed in [137]. The authors of [137] have used specific measures to evaluate and rank existing lightweight symmetric ciphers in terms of cost, speed, efficiency and balance criteria. Another review and classification on hardware implementations of elliptic curve cryptographic systems along with their applications has been presented in [125].

The trends in research on hardware implementation of lattice-based cryptographic schemes were studied in [254]. The importance of this research is induced by the role of lattice-based cryptography in post-quantum cryptography.

Another survey on hardware implementations of lightweight symmetric-key cryptography in resource-constrained devices has been reported in [174]. This research focuses on implementations based on $0.18\mu m$ CMOS technology.

A comparative study on FPGA implementations of cryptographic algorithms has been presented in [180]. Parameters such as operating frequency, throughput, the number of FPGA clock cycles and the number of slice registers have been used in this comparison.

A tutorial on recent research achievements related to the applications of hardware-oriented encryption, secret-sharing and multiparty computation (MPC) in cloud-based data outsourcing has been presented in [325].

The authors of [23] have conducted a survey on lightweight cryptography algorithms implemented in hardware to be used in IoT environments. In this survey, the algorithms and the implementations have been compared in terms of throughput and power consumption.

2.2 DESIGN

In this section, we study research works focusing on the design of cryptographic hardware and hardware-assisted cryptographic schemes. Most of these works have come up with some kind of implementation in addition to design. However, there are some research works that focus on implementation phases such as prototyping. The latter works will be reviewed in Section 2.3 along with a study on implementation challenges and objectives.

2.2.1 Cryptographic Primitives

Design methods proposed for cryptographic primitives such as key management, random number generation, hash functions and S-boxes are studied in the following.

Key Management

Key management plays a significant role in every cryptosystem. Several researchers have used hardware to design or improve key management frameworks and protocols. For example, a high-performance parallel architecture has been proposed in [176] to perform Supersingular Isogeny Key Encapsulation (SIKE), a class of post-quantum key encapsulation methods based on the Supersingular Isogeny Diffie-Hellman (SIDH) key exchange protocol. As another example, we can refer to the research reported in [98]. This paper presents the VHDL description of a hardware module for performing the Need2Knowreg system (N2K), which improves traditional access control methods based on public-key cryptography, to provide multi-user role-based access control. Furthermore, a low-cost, low-power key encryption hardware for securing functionally obfuscated DSP (digital signal processing) against removal attack has been proposed in [319].

Moreover, there are some proposals for attacking key management hardware modules as well as protecting them against attacks. For example, the authors of [364] have used fault injection analysis to propose a low-area key leakage trojan payload circuit for SM4, which is the Chinese standard for block cipher algorithms. Moreover, a hardware system based on Hardware Transactional Memories (HTMs) has been proposed in [196] in order to protect RSA keys against memory disclosure attacks. This system guarantees to abort suspicious memory transaction that may allow unauthorized access to keys stored in the memory in the form of plain text.

Random Number Generation

Three hardware architectures have been proposed in [297] for designing post-processing modules to be used in true random number generators. Post-processing modules designed based on the proposed architectures guarantee randomness using mathematical constructs called strong blenders. Using these three architectures, designers can manage tradeoffs among circuit-level design objectives. Quantum technology has been used by some researchers in order to design true random number generators. The authors of [230] proposed a quantum random bit generator using a single mobile charge on a coupled pair of quantum dots. True randomness of the output is guaranteed by quantum mechanics.

The authors of [58] have proposed a unified methodology capable of converting any probability distribution to a uniformly distributed random bit stream. The simple hardware implementation of this methodology makes it possible to improve the output of hardware random generators via some simple post-process. A hardware-implementable methodology with the opposite goal has been presented in [60]. The latter methodology can convert a uniform distribution created by a random number generator to an arbitrary probability distribution.

Some researchers have attempted at hardware implementation of random number generators that have previously been implemented in software. For example, a hardware implementation of the WELL (Well Equidistributed Long-period Linear) algorithm has been presented in [199]. The architecture proposed in this research is capable of dividing the WELL stream into an arbitrary number of independent parallel substreams, which helps in generating multiple simultaneous random numbers.

Hash Functions and Algorithms

Hash functions and algorithms are used in a variety of cryptosystems. Thus, implementing them in hardware can improve the performance and security of cryptosystems. This motivates a whole lot of research works. A flexible architecture for hardware design of Whirlpool hash family has been presented and evaluated in [170]. This architecture allows the designer to manage the tradeoffs among performance, area and security. The authors of [237] argued that existing hardware hashing modules can create bottlenecks in hardware-assisted cryptosystems due to their low throughput. They proposed a methodology to design high-throughput hardware circuits with dispensable area penalty for SHA-1 hash function. In [94], a CMOS design was proposed for a hardware hash unit that can be integrated into modern microprocessors and used in different applications including cryptography. A unified architecture for three different commercial MDC (Manipulation Detection Codes) hash primitives, namely MD5, SHA1 and RIPEMD160, has been presented in [107]. An ASIC implementation for the proposed architecture has been presented and evaluated in this paper.

The literature in this area comes with some research works focusing on the evaluation of existing hardware-implemented cryptographic hash functions. For example, the authors of [139] have evaluated and compared some well-known hardware hash modules with respect to their suitability for low-power embedded environments. The authors of [355] have shown how the rich functionality of modern general-purpose processors makes it possible to conduct an automated attack on self-hashing, which is a technique for verifying software integrity. The efficiency and generality of the attack scenario proposed in this paper defeats self-hashing, and shows that it cannot be considered as a dependable strategy for tamper resistance in modern computer systems. The hardware implementation efficiency of SHA-3 has been evaluated and compared with other hardware-implemented hash functions in [334] prior to being adopted as a standard by National Institute of Standard and Technology (NIST). Different hardware implementations of RadioGatún and irRUPT hash algorithms (which are candidates for replacing MD5 and SHA-1) have been evaluated and compared in [129]. Different hardware platforms such as ASIC and FPGA as well as different hardware circuit-level parameters such as area and throughput have been considered in this research.

Moreover, some researchers have focused on utilizing hardware capacities for the purpose of exploiting vulnerabilities in cryptographic hash functions. For example, the capabilities of reconfigurable hardware devices have been used in [65] for cryptanalysis of SHA-1.

S-Boxes

S-boxes are commonly used in several block ciphers as well as stream ciphers. This has motivated some research works focusing on the hardware implementation of S-boxes. For example, a compact FPGA-bases design for S-boxes has been presented in [80] to be used in Twofish cipher with 128-bit word and 128-192- and 256-bit key lengths. As another example, error detection schemes have been proposed in [160] for side-channel resistant S-boxes to be used in lightweight hardware block ciphers. The S-boxes designed in this research are protected against power analysis and fault analysis side-channel attacks via masking and reliability approaches, respectively.

2.2.2 Cryptographic Hardware

In the following, we review research on some special types of cryptographic hardware such as cryptographic hardware accelerators, cryptographic co-processors, cryptographic arithmetic modules, trusted platform modules, tamper-resistant devices and hardware security modules.

Cryptographic Hardware Accelerators (CHAs)

CHAs are used to implement computation-intensive cryptographic operations more efficiently than software codes run by CPU. They can be integrated into the SoC as a separate processor or integrated in a co-processor on the circuit board. Moreover, they can come on an extension circuit board connected to the mainboard or appear as a specific instruction set integrated to the CPU. A whole lot of research works have focused on the design of CHA. Some of these works are reviewed in the following.

A CHA for the RC-4 stream cipher and its variants has been designed in [161]. This CHA combines the capabilities of application-specific instruction set processors and application-specific ICs. The instruction set architecture integrated in this CHA aims at improving the performance via the reuse of combinational and sequential logic at various pipeline stages. Some FPGA-based CHAs for the RSA cipher have been designed and compared in [141]. Another FPGA-based CHA for the SSL/TLS cryptographic protocol has been proposed in [344]. The authors of [132] have designed a CHA for SNOW 3G and AES in order to be used in 3G Long-Term Evolution (LTE).

Some research works have focused on implementing cryptographic code on top of CPU-integrated CHAs. For example, the authors of [51] have implemented and evaluated some modules of IPSec using the CHA integrated in Intel XScale core. Some researchers have tried to use existing non-cryptographic coprocessors as CHAs. For example, the possibility of using GPUs (graphic processing units) as cryptographic accelerators for AES has been investigated in [222].

Some research works have added extra functionality to CHAs. As an example, one may refer to [277], wherein a CHA with FEC (forward error correction) capabilities has been designed. Others have examined the possibility of designing general-purpose CHAs to be used for different ciphers. For example, an attempt has been made in [52] to identify some common hotspot functions, which appear in different cryptosystems, and intensely occupy computation resources. In this paper, the identified functions have been integrated into a general-purpose CHA. Another general-purpose CHA has been designed in [88] for implementing S-boxes in symmetric ciphers.

Existing CHAs are vulnerable to some attacks, e.g., differential fault analysis attack. Some researchers have focused on developing methods for protecting CHAs. For example, a lightweight technique for protecting AES and SHA-1 hardware accelerators against differential fault analysis attack has been proposed in [190].

Different circuit-level design objectives such as power and throughput have been considered by CHA designers. For example, a low-power CHA for scalar multiplication in ECC over Galois

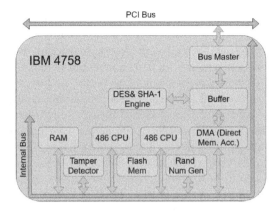

Figure 2.1 The schema of IBM 4758 PCI cryptographic co-processor (courtesy of [97]).

binary field has been designed in [157]. As another example, a high-throughput CHA for the HC-128 stream cipher has been presented in [54].

Cryptographic Co-processors

Cryptographic co-processors are processors specifically designed for encryption and related computations. They can be considered as CHAs equipped with a variety of protection features to prevent unauthorized data retrieval and circuit reverse engineering. They may provide some extra transaction processing capabilities in addition to encryption. For example, a smart card co-processor may implement transactions needed by smart cards. Figure 2.1 shows the block diagram of IBM 4758 PCI cryptographic co-processor.

Cryptographic co-processors have received a focus from researchers. A cryptographic co-processor for Galois field scalar multiplication has been designed in [248] to be used in ECC. This device can operate in both serial and parallel modes. Another cryptographic co-processor has been designed in [216] for performing Galois field multiplication in ECC. A co-processor featuring high inter-process communication (IPC) rate has been designed in [114] for digital signature verification using the Elliptic Curve Digital Signature Algorithm (ECDSA) according to the NIST B-233 standard.

While most cryptographic co-processors require the software to be adapted to their instruction set, some researchers have examined hardware-software codesign of cryptographic co-processors. For example, the authors of [102] have presented a framework for hardware-software codesign of a vector architecture for co-processors to be used in long precision modular multiplications. Another cryptographic co-processor based on codesign has been presented in [191]. The latter co-processor has a multi-core architecture aimed at achieving higher performance in server-based applications. Moreover, the hardware-software codesign approach has been taken in [173] to design a cryptographic co-processor for hyper-elliptic curve cryptography (HECC) based on MicroBlaze softcore processor and a Galois field co-processor.

Some researchers have designed cryptographic co-processors for specific applications and environments. As an example, we can refer to the RSA co-processor proposed in [134] for use in mobile applications such as cell phones and smart cards. On the other hand, there have been some attempts at the design of general-purpose cryptographic co-processors. For example, a cryptographic co-processor has been presented in [241] that can serve to different ciphers and different cryptographic elements such as key management, encryption and decryption. Another general-purpose cryptographic co-processor for AES, DES and SHA-1 has been designed in [103]. Moreover, some researchers have tried to add extra capabilities to cryptographic co-processors. As an example, one may refer to the co-processor presented in [70], which is equipped with message authentication capabilities in addition to encryption and decryption instructions integrated in it.

Different circuit-level design objectives such as performance [155] and area [122] have been considered in the design of cryptographic co-processors.

Cryptographic Arithmetic Modules (CAMs)

Cryptographic arithmetic modules, as suggested by the name, are used for high-performance execution of arithmetic computations in cryptosystem. They can be considered as special types of cryptographic co-processors that are usually designed as an enhancement to existing processors. Several research works have focused on the design of different types of CAMs. Some of these works are studied in the following.

- Galois Field Arithmetic Hardware

  Galois field and modular arithmetic computations are mostly used in ECC. This has motivated several research works on Galois field CAMs in recent decades [232] [393]. A CAM for $GF(2^{163})$ and $GF(2^{193})$ arithmetic computations has been designed in [162] to be used for ECC. This CAM is an enhancement to the Altera FPGA-based Nios II embedded processor. Another CAM for $GF(2^{192})$ arithmetic computations in ECC has been presented in [147]. The latter CAM has been designed for implementation on the Artix-7 FPGA from Xilinx. A more general Galois field CAM has been proposed in [27]. This CAM supports addition, subtraction, multiplication and inversion in all the five standard Galois fields recommended by NIST; $GF(2^{192})$, $GF(2^{224})$, $GF(2^{256})$, $GF(2^{384})$ and $GF(2^{521})$.

  Some Galois field CAMs perform only specific computation-intensive operations. As an example, one may refer to the CAM presented in [272], which performs a few variations of the Itoh-Tsujii Algorithm (ITA) for inversion over $GF(2^{233})$ and $GF(2^{233})$. Another CAM for Galois field inversion has been proposed in [62]. Moreover, the literature comes with CAMs that perform other Galois field operations such as multiplication [145] or division [342], or both.

  Developing formal methods for the description of Galois field arithmetic CAMs has been a concern for some researchers. A formal description method has been presented in [136] for this purpose. This method describes Galois field CAMs in the form of hierarchical graphs, where nodes represent subcircuits performing subfunctions, and edges represent data dependency between the subcircuits. Some research has been conducted on the hardware-software codesign of Galois field CAMs. For example, a dual-field CAM for ECC has been presented in [213] that is based on hardware-software codesign. This CAM is capable of being programmed to perform various point operations based on different algorithms.

- Hardware for Other Arithmetic Computations

  While most CAMs perform modular operations in Galois fields to be used in ECC, some of them support modular operations in other prime fields for application in RSA. For example, a CAM for modular multiplication in RSA has been

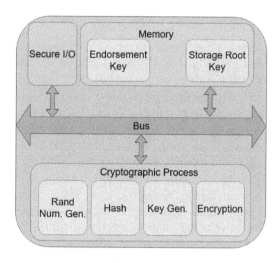

Figure 2.2 The schema of a typical plug-in card TPM.

designed in [368]. Another CAM has been proposed in [252] to perform modular exponentiation for application in RSA.

Trusted Platform Modules (TPMs)

TPMs are dedicated microcontrollers that are used to securely store cryptographic artifacts such as passwords, certificates and encryption keys. Figure 2.2 shows the schema of a typical TPM.

TPMs have been used in a variety of applications such as electronic voting [100] [99], digital forensics [116], software agent protection [322] and cyber-physical devices [135].

Tamper-Resistant Device (TRDs)

Tamper proofing refers to any methodology used to hinder, deter or detect unauthorized access to a device, assuming that the tampering party is not equipped with adequate knowledge or facilities. TRDs are commonly used for tamper proofing purposes in vehicles and similar environments. But they can never be considered as an ultimate security solution. Some researchers have studied different limitations of TRDs and investigated alternative solutions [57]. Others have added some additional hardware to improve the security of TRDs [365]. Moreover, some variants of TRDs

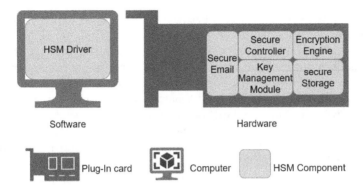

Figure 2.3 The schema of a typical plug-in card HSM.

such as user-centric TRD have been examined by the research community [22].

Hardware Security Modules (HSMs)

HSMs combine the functionality of cryptographic co-processors and TPMs. They usually perform encryption and decryption for digital signatures, protect and manage keys, and perform strong authentication. HSMs may be implemented as plug-in cards. Moreover, they can come in the form of external devices attached to network servers or individual computers. Figure 2.3 shows the schema of a typical pug-in card HSM

In the following, we review some research works focusing on different aspects of HSMs.

HSMs have been designed for a variety of applications. For example, an IaaS (infrastructure as a service) architecture based on HSMs has been presented in [321]. This architecture prevents malicious cloud administrators from affecting the security of guest virtual machines. As another example, the authors of [387] argued that storing the key (as a plain text) in memories makes encrypted file systems vulnerable to cold boot attacks. They proposed a key protection solution based on HSMs for the commonly used Linux Ext4 file system. In [286], an HSM has been designed for secure communications between IoT devices. Another HSM suitable for IoT communications has been designed in [310]. This HSM depends on process variations in the fabrication of memristor devices. The authors of [327] have proposed a framework based on HSM for securing the communications between a quad-copter and a ground station via encryption and authentication. In [164], an HSM has been proposed for secure channel establishment. In [142], an HSM has been designed for application in the three standard industrial buses mentioned in IEEE 1547-2018: Modbus, Distributed Network Protocol 3 (DNP3) and Smart Energy Profile 2.0 (SEP2). According to the standard, one of these buses must be used in each standardized distributed energy resources (DER) or power grid. As another example, one may refer to the research reported in [296]. This report first highlights scalability and security as critical requirements for an electronic voting system. Then it proposes a secure and scalable framework based on HSMs for electronic voting. Other researchers have used HSMs for other purposes such as recovering computers from malware attack [31].

Some research works have focused on designing circuits that perform part of the functionality of an HSM. As an example, we can refer to the ECC point multiplication hardware designed in [234] for application in HSMs. As another example, one may mention the circuit presented in [247], which provides the signature functionality of an HSM on top of available commodity hardware to support the operational signing workflow of Domain Name System Security Extensions (DNSSEC).

Some researchers have been interested in cryptanalysis of HSMs. For example, the authors of [187] have reported two security flaws in different implementations of HSMs. The first flaw is related to key deletion and the second may allow an unauthorized HSM to join an existing group of HSMs.

Different circuit-level and system-level design objectives such as FPGA implementation cost [273], power consumption [286] [310], scalability [296] and plug-and-play operation [31] have been considered in the design of HSMs.

Linear Feedback Shift Registers (LFSRs)

LFSRs are simple devices capable of being designed using a few flip-flops along with a few logical XOR gates, the layout of which is defined by a generating polynomial. There are two common representations of LFSRs, both of which are based on a shift register for keeping the state of the LFSR, along with a feedback loop, which controls the state transition. These representations are separately explained below.

1. **Fibonacci Representation:**

   This representation models the function of an LFSR $\mathcal{P}_n(G, M)$ by the state transition equation shown in Equation 2.1 over $GF(2)$.

   $$F_i(k+1) = \begin{cases} \sum_{t=1}^{n} G_i F_t(k) + M_k, & i = 1, \\ F_{i-1}(k), & i \in \{2, 3, \ldots, n\}. \end{cases} \quad (2.1)$$

   In equation 2.1, for every $i \in \{1, 2, \ldots, n\}$, $F_i(0)$ represents the initial value of the ith flip-flop (F_i), and $F_i(k)$ is the value stored in F_i at the end of the kth clock cycle for $k > 0$. In this representation, $G = \sum_{i=0}^{n} G_i x^i$ is referred to as the generating polynomial. In all real-world applications, $G_0 = G_n = 1$. Moreover, M_0 is the serial input available before the LFSR starts to work, and for $k > 0$, M_k is the serial input available at the kth clock cycle. Some LFSRs may not accept any serial input. This can be modeled by setting $\forall k \geq 0 :$ $M_k = 0$. In this case, we represent the LFSR by $\mathcal{P}_n(G, 0)$ or simply by $\mathcal{P}_n(G)$.

2. **Galois Representation:**

   In this representation, the state transition of $\mathcal{P}_n(G, M)$ is modeled by Equation 2.2.

   $$F_i(k+1) = \begin{cases} F_n(k) + M_k, & i = 1, \\ F_{i-1}(k) + G_{i-1} F_n(k), & i \in \{2, 3, \ldots, n\}. \end{cases} \quad (2.2)$$

   The notations used in Equation 2.2 are the same as those used in Equation 2.1.

   In both representations, n is referred to as the size of the LFSR, and the vector $\mathcal{S}^k(\mathcal{P}_n(G, M)) = [F_1(k), F_2(k), \ldots, F_n(k)]$ is called the kth state of the LFSR. Especially, $\mathcal{S}^0(\mathcal{P}_n(G, M)) = [F_1(0), F_2(0), \ldots, F_n(0)]$ is referred to as the initial state of the LFSR. Fibonacci and Galois representations of the architecture of an LFSR are shown in Figure 2.4.

   In the architecture shown in figure 2.4, $\oplus$ and $\odot$ represent $GF(2)$ addition and multiplication, respectively, which can be implemented in hardware using XOR and AND gates. Given a fixed generating polynomial, the $\odot$ operations will obviously be no longer

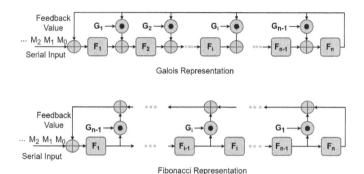

Figure 2.4 Galois and Fibonacci representations of the architecture of an LFSR of size n.

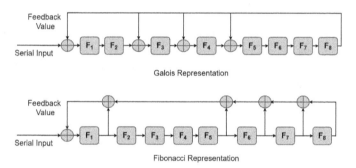

Figure 2.5 Galois and Fibonacci representations of an LFSR with generating polynomial $G = x^8 + x^4 + x^3 + x^2 + 1$.

needed. Moreover, in an implementation with a fixed generating polynomial, the output of each $\odot$ operation will be equal to 0 if its G input is 0. This eliminates the need for the corresponding $\oplus$ operation. As an example, the Fibonacci and Galois representations of an LFSR with generating polynomial $G = x^8 + x^4 + x^3 + x^2 + 1$ are shown in Figure 2.5.

If we interpret each state of the LFSR as an integer number, an LFSR with n flip-flops and a primitive generating polynomial G guarantees to generate $2^n - 1$ different numbers $\{1, 2, \ldots, 2^n - 1\}$ in each $2^n - 1$ consecutive clock cycles by an order $r_0, r_1, \ldots, r_j, \ldots, r_{2^n-1}$, which depends on G. This property enables LFSRs to play significant roles in a variety of cryptographic primitives such as designing the pseudorandom number generation [357] [377] [350] and hashing [178] as well as key stream generation in stream ciphers [391] [96]. Moreover, they have been used in some cryptography-related applications such as steganography [148]. In the following, we briefly review existing research works focusing on different aspects of designing LFSRs for application in cryptography.

Some research works have focused on the use of LFSRs in the design of random number generators. For example, the authors of [350] have used LFSRs to design and test a random number generator for application in stream ciphers. Another LFSR-based random number generator has been designed and tested in [226]. The authors of [158] have designed an LFSR-based random number generator specialized for application in the classical Playfair cipher.

Some researchers have investigated the application of LFSRs in stream ciphers. For example, the authors of [391] have used LFSRs to improve the resistance of a stream cipher based on Feedback with Carry Shift Registers (FCSRs) - proposed in [30] - against chosen ciphertext attacks. In [324], the authors have introduced the notion of complex LFSR. Then they have designed a single reconfigurable complex LFSR that can replace the three LFSRs used in the A5-1 stream cipher or the four LFSRs used in A5-2. Some researchers have suggested key-dependent LFSR configurations in order to make stream ciphers more resistant to algebraic attacks [68].

There are some research works wherein LFSR-based random number generators have been designed and used in stream ciphers. As an example, the authors of [111] have proposed an LFSR-based random number generator, and used it in two lightweight chaotic stream ciphers based on Skew Tent Map (STM) and a modified variant of logistic map. Another LFSR-based random number generator has been designed and used in stream ciphers by the authors of [244].

LFSRs can be used to design Galois field multipliers as well as dividers, both of which are used in stream ciphers. The authors of [375] have compared multipliers based on stream ciphers with those based on dividers. Moreover, they have proposed a framework for converting LFSR-based dividers to multipliers.

PUFs

PUF is a megatrend in research on cryptographic hardware and hardware-oriented cryptography. In recent years, weak [32] and strong [221] [284] PUFs as well as static [197] and dynamic [376] ones have been used in several cryptographic mechanisms such as encryption [284], authentication [159] [285], key generation [165] and software protection [376]. PUFs have been used in a variety of environments from IoT [285] and industrial control [71] to automotive industry [284] and smart grids [159]. In the following, we briefly review some of the most recent research works focusing on PUF in order to highlight the directions of the technology and some popular research topics in this area.

There are a whole lot of PUFs designed on the basis of ring oscillators. As an example, one may refer to the PUF designed in [200]. This PUF utilizes a delay cell topology featuring an adjusted signal slope, which helps amplify the impact of device variability on delay mismatch in order to improve stability. As an other mechanism aimed at improving stability, the mentioned PUF makes use of an online calibration system that extracts in situ PUF delay information and reconfigures the stage interconnects. Some PUFs have been designed using the unavoidable process variations in CMOS technology. For example, the authors of [32] have designed a PUF using a Wheatstone bridge. The bridge uses positive and negative feedback simultaneously in order to magnify the small process variations. The output signal of this PUF is electrical impedance, and features a bimodal distribution. Different kinds of volatile and non-volatile memories have been used to design PUFs. For example, an SRAM-based PUF has been designed in [208], and the authors of [61] have introduced another PUF based on non-volatile memories. In [221], the intrinsic variations in the nonlinear static characteristics and leakage currents of ReRAM (resistive RAM) circuits have been used to design a PUF. This PUF employs passive crossbar circuits to amplify the variations. Several other kinds of devices have been used to design PUFs. As an example, we can mention the PUF designed in [197] using a sub-threshold inverter along with a transistor-based voltage regulation scheme. As another example, one may refer to the PUF proposed in [335] on the basis of a linear optical device containing Mach-Zehnder interferometers.

The PUF designed in [221] uses a leakage injection technique based on an electrically isolated portion of the crossbar array in order to improve robustness. Moreover, a key booking scheme has been used in the designed of the PUF, aimed at improving reliability across a wide range of operation temperatures and further increasing the density of the circuit via reducing error correcting overheads. This PUF has been demonstrated to be highly resistant to machine learning attacks. In addition to robustness, some other system-level goals have been followed by PUF designers. Among these goals, we can mention variation resilience [200], reliability [165] and attack resilience [288].

Different implementation approaches and objectives have been considered by researchers while designing PUFs. For example, intrinsic PUFs are implemented in software and use the variations of existing hardware components without any modification to the hardware. An intrinsic PUF based on GPUs has been designed in [101].

PUFs may feature uniqueness [197], randomness [32] or both of them [221]. Different measures such as native instability [32] [197] and BER (bit error rate) [221] [197] are used to evaluate PUFs. They may be implemented using ASICs [32] or CMOS technology [197] [200].

2.2.3 Hardware-Assisted Ciphers

Different kinds of ciphers have been designed with the assistance of cryptographic hardware. These ciphers can be classified from different points of view as follows.

Block Ciphers and Stream Ciphers

Several research works have focused on designing both block ciphers and stream ciphers using cryptographic hardware. Some of these works are reviewed in the following.

- Block Ciphers:

  In recent years, hardware-based design of block ciphers has been of interest to researchers [308]. Hardware-based block ciphers have been used in different applications, environments and platforms such as image encryption [38], wireless sensors [172] and multicore processors [195].

  Some researchers have designed cryptographic elements to be used in stream ciphers. As an example, we can refer to the S-box designed in [207] for application in RoadRunneR block cipher. Moreover, some research works have proposed comprehensive hardware designs for entire block ciphers such as CLEFIA [289], MISTY1 [382] [169], KASUMI [167] [382], RC6 block cipher (testable) [224], Camellia block cipher [59], LED and HIGHT [336], PRESENT [189] [268], FeW [255], Rijndael [85] and KLEIN block cipher [18].

In the hardware design for block ciphers, several circuit-level objectives such as performance [167], testability [224] and area [59] [169] [311] have been considered by researchers. Furthermore, system-level objectives such as fault tolerance [18] and reliability [336] have been considered in research works focusing on hardware design for block ciphers.

Lightweight hardware design for block ciphers has received a research focus. For example, a hardware platform has been proposed in [201] for four lightweight block ciphers, namely Piccolo, PRESENT, LED and PRINTcipher. However, lightweight implementations bring about some security problems such as vulnerability against hardware trojans. For example, the authors of [260] have designed a hardware trojan to attack a lightweight implementation of Piccolo block cipher.

In addition to the design of new hardware-based block ciphers or new hardware for existing block ciphers, some researchers have compared existing hardware block ciphers. For example, some ISO/IEC 29192-2 adaptable hardware block ciphers have been compared in [127]. Moreover, some research works have focused on comparing hardware and software implementations of block ciphers [86].

- Stream Ciphers:

  In addition to block ciphers, several researchers have proposed hardware circuits as well as hardware-based architectures for stream ciphers in their recent works [347] [348].

  Some research works have presented novel hardware-assisted stream ciphers. As an example, we can refer to the research reported in [369]. In this research, the authors have proposed an area-efficient family of hardware-implementable random number generators and used them for key stream generation in a novel stream cipher. Other research works have focused on efficient hardware design for existing stream ciphers. For example, a hardware design featuring variable-length key has been proposed for RC4 in [168]. This design supports 8 to 128 bits long keys. Another architecture for hardware implementation of RC4 has been presented in [123]. This architecture makes use of pipelining and loop unfolding techniques to achieve a high degree of parallelism. Salsa20 is another stream cipher frequently consider by researchers for hardware implementation. For example, hardware designs for Salsa20 and its successor ChaCha have been presented in [128]. The design makes use of Rumba, which is a compression scheme used for hashing functions. Another architecture for hardware implementation of Salsa20 (as well as Phelix) has been proposed in [378]. The authors of [225] have proposed a hardware design for Grain stream cipher. They have utilized five different techniques, namely internal pipelining, authentication section isolation, multi-frequency implementation, Fibonacci-to-Galois LFSR transformation and pre-outputs function simplification, in order to achieve higher performance. Hardware designs have been proposed for several other stream ciphers. One may refer, for example, to Hermes [171].

Hardware-implemented stream ciphers have been targeted for several platforms, environments and applications. For example, a hardware-implemented chaotic stream cipher has been proposed in [37] for application in color image encryption. The stream cipher designed in [37] employs the processed chaotic output in order to mask and diffuse input pixels using multiple stages of bit permutation and XORing. As another example, we can refer to the hardware design for RC4 proposed in [261], which is targeted for WEP (wired equivalent privacy). The authors of [261] argued that WEP suffers a limitation caused by the adaptation of RC4 stream cipher. Their proposed hardware design aims at alleviating this limitation.

Hardware design of lightweight stream ciphers has been of interest for some researchers. For example, a hardware architecture has been proposed in [363] for implementing PUF-FIN, which is originally a lightweight stream cipher. Other researchers have focused on lightweight hardware design for existing stream ciphers that are originally not lightweight. For example, a lightweight design for RC4 has been proposed in [346] to be used in image encryption. The mentioned cipher depends on a two-dimensional CA (cellular automata) for key stream generation.

Different circuit-level design objectives have been considered by researchers while designing hardware-based stream ciphers. Among these objectives, one may refer to performance [123] [171], hardware complexity [259] and area [369].

In addition to hardware design for stream ciphers, some researchers have compared existing hardware implementations of stream ciphers. For example, FPGA-based implementations of five well-known stream ciphers, namely A5/1, E0, RC4, W7 and Helix, have been compared in [106]. A5/1, E0 and RC4 have been adopted by several security standards. The other two ciphers are considered as good choices for GSM and other communication environments.

Symmetric-Key Ciphers and Public-Key Ciphers

As mentioned before, cryptosystems can be classified in different ways. For example, on the basis of the key generation scheme, cryptosystems are divided into two main categories: symmetric-key cryptosystems and public-key cryptosystems. Both categories have been considered for hardware-assisted design. In the following, we review some related research works.

- Symmetric-Key Cryptography:

  Designing hardware for symmetric-key cryptography has been of interest to some researchers. For example, the authors of [80] and [79] have proposed compact hardware-implementable S-boxes to be used in Twofish. As another example, we may refer to the hardware design proposed by the authors of [320] for SEED, which is a Korean standard 128-bit symmetric block cipher.

- Public-Key Cryptography:

  Like the case of symmetric-key ciphers, some researchers have worked on the design of novel hardware-assisted public-key ciphers. As an example, one can mention the cryptosystem proposed in [154]. Other researchers have designed hardware modules to be used in existing public-key ciphers. For example, the authors of [358] have proposed a hardware module that performs high-radix modular exponentiation for application in existing public-key ciphers.

Traditional and Emerging Cryptographic Paradigms

Hardware modules and architectures have been used in the design and realization of cryptosystems based on traditional paradigms such as ECC, lattice-based cryptography and randomized cryptography as well as emerging paradigms such as homomorphic encryption, pairing-based cryptography, attribute-based encryption, identity-based encryption, DNA-based cryptography and postquantum cryptography. In the following, we briefly review some research works related to these topics.

- Traditional Paradigms:

    Hardware-assisted design of cryptosystems based on traditional paradigms has been the focus of several research works, some of which are studied below.

    - ECC:

        The authors of [390] have designed a hardware-implementable Montgomery modular multiplication method along with a hardware-assisted mechanism for accelerating point operations in elliptic curve cryptosystems. A reconfigurable hardware architecture for the design of ECC combinational logic circuits has been designed in [282]. This architecture is supported by a genetic algorithm in order to reduce vulnerability against non-invasive side-channel analysis attacks such as power, timing, electromagnetic, visible light and acoustic analysis attacks. The authors of [312] have proposed a hardware architecture that integrates ECC and lossless compression in a single chip. In this architecture, the input data is compressed using a dictionary-based lossless data compressor before being encrypted. Then either ECIES (Elliptic Curve Integrated Encryption Scheme) or ECDSA (Elliptic Curve Digital Signature Algorithm) can be applied to the compressed data for encryption or digital signature, respectively. The authors of [314] have focused on Curve25519 and Curve448, which have been suggested by RFC 7748 to be implemented in software and used by next-generation TLS. They proposed an architecture for hardware implementation of both ciphers. In this architecture, robustness against side-channel attacks has been considered as a primary design goal.

- Lattice-Based Cryptography:
  A few researchers have proposed hardware for lattice-based cryptography. Some related research works have been reviewed in [254].
- Randomized Cryptography:
  Some research works have designed hardware for randomized cryptography. For example, an area-efficient hardware-implementable randomized cryptographic scheme has been presented in [313] for the purpose of secure key exchange.

• Emerging Cryptographic Paradigms

  Emerging cryptographic paradigms are taking advantage of cryptographic hardware like the case of traditional paradigms. In the following, we review some research works that help outline the directions of research on the use of hardware in cutting-edge cryptography.

  - Homomorphic Encryption:
    Hardware implementation of homomorphic [166] [20] and somewhat homomorphic encryption [238] has received a research focus in recent years. The first full hardware design for an FHE (fully homomorphic encryption) scheme was presented in [87] for the Gentry-Halevi scheme. This design uses a novel high-performance multiplier based on the Schonhage-Strassen multiplication algorithm along with some optimizations such as spectral techniques as well as a pre-computation strategy.
    Some researchers have focused on designing hardware-software codesign for homomorphic encryption. For example, hardware-software codesign techniques have been used in [239] in order to design an accelerator for performing the Karatsuba algorithm instead of FFT (fast fourier transform) in the Fan-Vercauteren (FV) homomorphic encryption scheme. Moreover, using hardware-software codesign techniques, the authors of [235] have designed a parametric Number Theoretic Transform (NTT) hardware generator that takes arithmetic configurations and the number of processing elements as inputs, and produces an efficient NTT hardware to be used in homomorphic encryption.

- Pairing-Based Cryptography:
Hardware design for pairing-based cryptography has been considered by several researchers. For example, the authors of [115] have proposed a hardware design for pairing-based cryptography. They demonstrated that their design is robust against side-channel attacks. Especially, designing lightweight hardware for pairing-based cryptography has been of interest to some researchers. As an example, we can mention the high-speed, low-power hardware proposed in [309] for Montgomery multiplication to be used in cryptosystems based on Ate pairing. This multiplier is resistant to simple power analysis (SPA) and differential power analysis (DPA) attacks. Different circuit-level design objectives such as power [309] and performance [309] have been considered by researchers while designing hardware for pairing-based cryptography.

- Attribute-Based Encryption (ABE):
A few hardware designs have been proposed for ABE schemes. As an example, one may refer to the low-power FPGA-based ABE design presented in [14], which targets IoT applications.

- Identity-Based Encryption (IBE)
In addition to ABE, some research works have focused on hardware design for IBE schemes. For example, a hardware module has been designed in [118] for performing the computations required by Tate pairing to be used in IBE schemes. Moreover, a cryptographic co-processor for Tate pairing with applications in IBE cryptosystems has been designed in [41].

- Post-Quantum Cryptography:
Hardware design for post-quantum cryptography is a recent research focus [374]. Some researchers have presented hardware-implementable primitives for post-quantum cryptography. For example, the authors of [19] have proposed hardware for QKE (quantum key exchange) and some other post-quantum cryptographic primitives. Moreover, the authors of [217] have presented a hardware-implementable methodology for deriving Boolean functions to map a uniformly random bit sequence into a value from a discrete distribution. They

demonstrated how their proposed hardware can be used in post-quantum cryptography. Other researchers have proposed full hardware designs for post-quantum cryptosystems. As an example, we can mention the high-performance hardware architecture presented in [29] for Round5 post-quantum cryptosystem. This architecture supports public-key encryption as well as key encapsulation.

Hardware-software codesign of post-quantum cryptographic algorithms and primitives has been of interest to several researchers. For example, a hardware-software codesign approach has been presented in [256] for the design of NTT modules to be used in post-quantum cryptography. Another hardware-software codesign has been proposed for NTRUEncrypt post-quantum cryptography algorithm in [95]. Moreover, hardware-software codesign has been applied to three lattice-based post-quantum key encapsulation mechanisms in [75].

- DNA-Based Cryptography:

  The literature in the area of cryptography comes with a few research works focusing on hardware design for DNA-based cryptography. For example, the authors of [150] have proposed hardware for DNA-based encryption and decryption as well as DNA-based key generation.

2.2.4   Automatic Design and Synthesis

There are a few research works that have focused on automatic design and synthesis of hardware for cryptography. As an example of research works focusing on automatic hardware design, one may mention the research reported in [370]. In this research, an EDA (electronic design automation) tool has been designed in order to generate some basic building blocks for cryptographic hardware in the form of VHDL codes. As an example of synthesis, we can mention the systematic approach presented in [229] for the purpose of fault-tolerant hardware design for cryptosystems. The authors of [229] have successfully applied their proposed approach to some LFSR-based stream ciphers such as A5/1 (adopted by GSM), E0 (used in Bluetooth), RC4 (suggested by WEP) and W7.

2.2.5 Design Objectives

Performance has been considered as a critical circuit-level design objective in research on hardware-assisted cryptography [177] [262]. Performance has been measured in terms of different metrics such as latency [84] and throughput [276]. Different techniques such as parallelism [250] [41] and pipelining [117] [318] have been used to achieve high performance. In addition to performance, area [388] and resource efficiency [206] have been considered by some researchers. Moreover, some research works have focused on power consumption [274] and energy efficiency [331].

In addition to circuit-level design objectives, system-level objectives such as fault tolerance [152] have been studied in some research works. Furthermore, some researchers have examined the tradeoffs among different objectives [55].

2.3 IMPLEMENTATION

In this section, we study the research reports that have focused on implementation-related processes such as prototyping. Moreover, we study implementation technologies used in hardware-assisted cryptography as well as the related implementation objectives and challenges.

2.3.1 Prototyping

Prototypes for cryptographic hardware and hardware-based ciphers have been presented in a few research works, among which we may mention the research reported in [108]. The authors of this paper argued that traditional verification techniques are not sufficient for delivering bug-free first-pass silicon, and designers are turning to pre-silicon prototypes in order to address this challenge. They proposed a unified hardware architecture for the purpose of designing hardware for MD5, SHAI and RIPEMD160. They presented an FPGA prototype of the hardware built on the basis of their proposed architecture. Moreover, a CMOS prototype of a hardware random number generator has been presented in [265]. Another FPGA-based prototype has been presented in [163] for a CAM that implements cryptographic algorithms used by SSL/TLS including AES-256 symmetric encryption, SHA-2 hashing and RSA-2048 public-key cryptography.

2.3.2 Implementation Technologies

In the following, we study technologies used for implementing hardware-assisted cryptosystems.

FPGA Implementation

FPGA has been widely used in cryptographic hardware implementation. To exemplify the applications of FPGAs in the implementation of hardware-assisted cryptosystems, one may refer to the following.

In [215], FPGAs have been used in the implementation of hardware architecture that aims at protecting secret keys against side-channel attacks. The authors of [188] have used this technology in two lightweight implementations of PRESENT stream cipher. A hybrid cryptographic hardware has been implemented using FPGA in [326]. This hardware combines RSA with AES in a way that RSA is used to encrypt the AES key. An FPGA implementation has been proposed in [269] for Lehmer random number generator, which belongs to the class of multiplicative linear congruential pseudorandom number generators.

In addition to implementation of cryptographic hardware, FPGAs have been used for implementing attacks on cryptographic systems. For example, the authors of [45] have used FPGAs to implement an attack scenario against a secure electronic election system.

CMOS Implementation

CMOS is another widely used technology for the implementation of cryptographic hardware. For example, this technology has been used to implement a random number generator in IBM POWER7+^{TM} processor [202]. The authors of [21] have proposed and implemented a novel cipher for application in ad hoc networks. Their proposed cipher combines data sealing with RAC (random addressing cryptography). Moreover, a 64-bit block, 128-bit key, dynamically reconfigurable hardware-based cipher has been implemented by the authors of [242]. This cipher has been dedicatedly designed for cryptographic applications in mobile computing.

ASIC Implementation

A few researchers have used ASICs to implement cryptographic hardware. For example, the authors of [369] have used ASICs to implement a low-area hardware-oriented random number generator that can be considered as a variant of Panama. Panama is a pseudorandom number generator designed to achieve high performance in software implementations. There are hardware implementations for Panama, but none of them is efficient in terms of area. While all existing hardware-oriented lattice-based cryptosystems have been implemented using FPGAs, the authors of [264] have studied the challenges and considerations of implementing a lattice-based cipher using ASICs.

TTL Implementation

A few cryptographic hardware modules have been implemented in TTL technology. As an example, one may refer to the implementation of the random number generator reported in [275]. This random number generator can generate both uniform and Gaussian distributions.

Combinations of Technologies

Some researchers have used more than one technology for implementing hardware-based ciphers. For example, the authors of [378] have used both ASIC and FPGA for the realization of both Salsa20 and Phelix stream ciphers. They have compared the area and throughput of all implementations.

2.3.3 Implementation Goals and Challenges

In this subsection, we study the implementation goals and challenges considered by researchers while implementing cryptographic hardware and hardware-assisted cryptosystems.

Embedded Implementation

The literature in the area of hardware-oriented cryptography comes with several embedded implementations. To mention a few, one can refer to the realizations reported in [43] and [333]. In [43], three different embedded implementations have been presented for AES. The authors of this paper have evaluated and compared the resistance of their proposed implementations against side-channel attacks. The authors of [333] have presented embedded hardware implementations for a block cipher, a stream cipher and a hash function.

Lightweight Implementation

In addition to embedded implementations, some researchers have focused on lightweight implementations for cryptographic hardware. For example, in [330], a lightweight implementation has been proposed for a stream cipher to be used in IoT edge devices. This stream cipher features side-channel attack resistance in addition to its lightweight design. Moreover, we can mention another lightweight stream cipher implemented in [346] for application in color image encryption.

Testability

Testability is another challenge in the design of hardware for cryptographic applications. As an example, one may refer to the BIST (built-in self-test) system designed in [223] for application in RC6 cipher.

Reconfigurability

A few researchers have focused on reconfigurable implementations for cryptographic hardware. As an example, we can mention the reconfigurable parallel cryptographic co-processor implemented by the authors of [251]. This co-processor has been designed to dedicatedly perform LFSR operations.

Reversibility

Reversibility - as an implementation goal - has been considered by several researchers in the area of hardware cryptography. Reversible hardware design for cryptographic applications was first proposed in [343]. The authors of this paper implemented a reversible cryptographic co-processor. Reversibility is especially useful for designing quantum circuit as well as cryptographic modules robust against power analysis attacks [36]. The authors of [332] have proposed a reversible LFSR for applications in cryptography.

Other Goals and Challenges

In addition to embedded implementation, lightweight implementation, testability, reconfigurability and reversibility, some other implementation goals and challenges have been considered by the research community. To mention a few, one may refer to asynchronous implementation [341], glitch-free implementation [204] and uniformly switching implementation [227].

2.4 EVALUATION

In the following, we review the research works focusing on the evaluation of cryptographic hardware. Some of these works have evaluated the security of cryptographic hardware. Others have focused on simulation and performance benchmarking.

2.4.1 Security Evaluation

Researchers have used hardware trojans, attack scenarios and cryptanalysis techniques for the evaluation of hardware cryptographic systems. Some related research works are studied in the following.

Hardware Trojans

Hardware trojans have been widely used for the purpose of security evaluation of hardware-based cryptographic modules and systems. To this end, different types of trojans have been proposed, among which one may refer to cipher-destroying and key-emitting trojans [179] as well as data-leaking trojans [291].

Several researchers have focused on the design of trojans in cryptographic hardware. For example, the authors of [210] have designed two trojans for the purpose of leaking the key from an IC that implements AES. The injection of trojans has been another topic of interest to researchers in the area of hardware-oriented cryptography. For example, the authors of [182] have examined the injection of two different trojans in cryptographic hardware modules. These trojans are activated with a very low probability under a slightly reduced supply voltage.

Preventing the injection of trojans is a countermeasure considered in some studies. For example, in [373], FHE has been suggested as an approach to preventing the implantation of a trojan in a cryptographic hardware.

Detection is another common countermeasure against trojans. For example, a trojan detection method for cryptographic hardware has been proposed in [367] that calculates temporal features of IDDT (quiescent power supply current) and IDDQ (transient power supply current) signals, then applies mRMR (Minimum-Redundancy Maximum-Relevance) algorithm to choose the feature subset, and finally uses Mahalanobis distance calculation to detect trojans. As another example, the authors of [211] have presented a concurrent hardware trojan detection scheme for wireless cryptographic ICs. This method is based on extracting a side-channel fingerprint and evaluating the fingerprint using trained-on-chip neural classifier. Several other approaches have been used for the detection of trojans in cryptographic hardware. Some researchers have studied methods for triggering trojans in order to facilitate it to detect them [63]. Some research works have proposed the use of side-channel analysis to detect trojans [12]. Others have introduced testable cryptographic that can detect trojans in testing time [246].

Some researchers have investigated both the injection and detection of trojans. For example, the authors of [42] have studied the injection of trojans as well as identifying them in IP (intellectual property) blocks.

In addition to design, injection, prevention, triggering and detection, some studies have explored methods for neutralizing trojans in cryptographic hardware. For example, a hardware dithering method for neutralization of trojans in cryptographic ICs has been proposed in [156]. This method makes the operating point of an IC an unpredictable moving target during run time. This restricts the ability of a trojan to exploit the process variation margins.

Attacks

Some researchers have designed attack scenarios for cryptanalysis of cryptographic hardware. For example, the authors of [236] have conducted and reported a chosen plain text attack on a hardware implementation of AES. A fault injection attack scenario has been designed in [279] for attacking cryptographic hardware. On the other hand, some research works have proposed approaches for attack-tolerant cryptographic hardware implementation. To mention a few, one may refer to the researches reported in [229], [345] and [345].

Cryptanalysis

Cryptanalysis has been widely used by researchers in order to evaluate the security of hardware-assisted ciphers. A variety of approaches have been proposed for this paper. To mention a few, one may refer to power analysis [78] and differential fault analysis [366] as well as guess and determine analysis [353].

Well-known security weaknesses of lightweight hardware-assisted cryptosystems have motivated some research works that focus on the cryptanalysis of these implementations. For example, the lightweight cipher PRESENT has been cryptanalyzed in [280]. As another example, one can mention the research reported in [385]. The authors of this paper have proposed a method for side-channel cryptanalysis of lightweight unrolled cryptographic hardware, which aim at encryption/decryption in a single clock cycle. Moreover, an open-source platform has been proposed in [15] for evaluating the resistance of lightweight authenticated ciphers against power analysis attacks.

Vulnerability Exploits

A few researchers have exploited the vulnerabilities of existing cryptographic hardware, and reported the results. For example, some vulnerabilities in a reconfigurable hardware implementation of SHA-1 have been exploited in [66].

2.4.2 Simulation and Performance Benchmarking

Benchmarking of hardware-based cryptographic modules has received attention from a few researchers. For example, the authors of [105] have presented an open-source set of tools for automated benchmarking of cryptographic hardware. Moreover, some researchers have focused on the simulation of cryptographic hardware. For example, the authors of [144] have reported the simulation results obtained from a hardware implementation of a scalar multiplication algorithm used in ECC over GF(2163). As another example, one may refer to the simulation results obtained from a randomized cryptographic algorithm, which have been reported in [83].

CHAPTER 3

PUFs in Industry, Education Programs and Books

In this chapter, we first present a brief historical review of physically unclonable functions (PUFs). Then, we study the approach of the industry, education programs and publishers towards PUFs.

3.1 HISTORICAL BACKGROUND

The initial research on exploiting the physical properties of disordered systems for authentication purposes were reported in [39], [328] and [329]. Later on, these properties were used to present an authentication scheme for memory cards [249]. Systems with similar ideas were named POWFs (physical one-way functions) in [270]. From 2010 to 2013, PUFs got a focus from the smart card market as a means of providing silicon fingerprints and generating unique cryptographic keys [67].

3.2 PUF IN INDUSTRY

PUFs have found important applications in the FPGA industry and commercial products. For example, Xilinx Zynq UltraScale+ [11] and Altera Stratix 10 [1] use PUFs as a secure alternative to battery-backed storage of secret keys.

Moreover, industrial groups are producing commercial PUFs for several other applications. For example, Intrinsic-ID produces PUFs for use in IoT devices as well as other embedded devices [2]. Synopsis has used Intrinsic-ID PUFs in its ARC EM processors [8].

3.3   PUF IN EDUCATION PROGRAMS

PUFs have been of interest to universities and academic institutes. For example, several universities have presented related courses and lectures. To mention a few, one may refer to MIT [4], Stanford [5] and Technical University of Munich [3].

Many universities have formed research groups and labs that work on PUFs. Among these universities, we can mention Yale [9] and National University of Singapore [7].

Many universities such as Iowa State University [240], University of Massachusetts at Amherst [354] and University of Minnesota at Twin Cities [175] have defined and accomplished theses focusing on PUFs.

Moreover, several universities including Northern Arizona University [6] and New York University [10] have designed, implemented and patented new PUFs.

3.4   PUF IN BOOKS

In recent years, some publishers such as Springer [124] and Morgan & Claypool [359] have published comprehensive and useful books that study different aspects of PUFs.

- The authors of [124] start with an overview of security threats on embedded systems and existing countermeasures. They continue with a discussion on design and evaluation methods for PUFs as well as some sample hardware implementations. They study the related reliability challenges and the state-of-the-art mitigation approaches such as those based on error correction codes and/or pre-processing techniques. Moreover, they present a tutorial on the security threats facing PUF technology, including modeling attacks using machine learning algorithms, side-channel analysis and physical attacks along with some possible countermeasures and defense mechanisms. They discuss some practical applications such as secure cryptographic key generation and storage, hardware-assisted security protocols, low-cost secure sensors, anti-counterfeit integrated circuits and anti-tamper hardware.

- Different classes of optical attacks, especially optical contactless probing, laser fault injection and photonic emission analysis are studied in [339]. The susceptibility of intrinsic PUF implementations based on reconfigurable hardware to optical semi-invasive attacks from the chip backside is investigated in this book. It also presents a feasibility study on these attacks. Furthermore, it demonstrates how the outputs of a PUF can be predicted, manipulated or directly probed without an impact on its behavior. This book argues that PUFs are not tamper-evident in their current configuration, and therefore, they cannot raise the security level of key storage by their own. It introduces existing remedies to PUFs' security-related shortcomings, which make them resistant to optical side-channel and optical fault attacks. Lastly, a prototype tamper-evident sensor is introduced for detecting optical contactless probing attempts.

- Machine learning (ML) attacks on ICs using PUFs are investigated in [109]. Some mathematical proofs are presented in this book to clarify the vulnerability of various PUF types such as Arbiter, XOR Arbiter, ring oscillator and bistable ring PUFs to machine learning attacks. This book presents a generic framework for the assessment of these PUFs based on two main approaches. First, fit-for-purpose mathematical representations of the mentioned types of PUFs are established in order to reflect their physical behavior. These representations reintroduce notions and formalizations already familiar to the machine learning research community in order to give a better understanding of the feasibility of machine learning attacks against PUFs. Second, polynomial time machine learning algorithms are explored, which can learn a PUF of the mentioned types.

- A review and classification of methods for constructing PUFs, with a focus on intrinsic PUFs, is presented in [218]. This book presents algorithmic descriptions for PUFs along with formal frameworks for deploying PUFs and similar physical primitives in cryptographic reductions. This book studies the multitude of the physical construction of PUFs and their representative physical and algorithmic properties as well as the techniques required to deploy them in security applications.

- An overview of various PUF-related topics providing theoretical background and application details is presented in [48]. This book focuses on the practical considerations of designing PUF hardware, especially microelectronic PUF circuits. The authors of this book discuss circuit-based methods for minimizing error rate. Moreover, they provide sample PUF circuits along with testing and measurement results. Furthermore, pre-selection techniques are presented in this book for the purpose of error rate reduction.

- The authors of [359] focus on PUFs as emerging and promising solutions for establishing trust in embedded systems with minimal hardware requirements. The integration of PUFs into secure and efficient cryptographic protocols used in embedded systems is one of the main focuses of this book. Specifically, the integration of PUFs into lightweight device authentication and attestation schemes is studied in this book.

In addition to the aforementioned books, there are several books that discuss PUFs as part of their contents [351] [292].

CHAPTER 4

Preliminary Discussions

In this chapter, we first review existing surveys on PUFs, then explain the motivations for the work of this book despite existing surveys and, finally, discuss the methodology used in this research.

4.1 RELATED WORKS: A SURVEY ON SURVEYS

In this section, we briefly review existing surveys in a chronological order.

2010: A survey on the applications of PUF in hardware authentication was presented in [90]. This report presented some guidelines for choosing among existing types of PUFs according to the application. A general taxonomy on PUFs was presented in [220]. The authors of this research work presented a terminology for the area, and studied different applications of PUFs. Moreover, they suggested some directions for future research in this area.

2012: A survey on PUFs and their applications was reported in [360]. This report covers attacks on PUFs, implementation issues, evaluation and applications in cryptographic protocols. Furthermore, the security model of PUF-based systems has been examined in this research.

A review and evolution study on PUFs with an emphasis on the strength-based classification was presented in [303].

2014: A study on features and implementation issues of PUFs along with their applications, especially applications in security protocols, was reported in [304]. This research specifically focused on a comparison between weak PUFs and strong PUFs. The authors of this report presented a very short history of PUF and its origins. Modeling attacks on PUFs were reviewed in [305]. In this research, the vulnerabilities in PUFs that make modeling attacks applicable were studied along with the machine learning algorithms used by these attacks. The authors of this report studied successful attacks and outlined some future research topics related to modeling attacks.

Silicon and ring oscillator PUFs were studied in [389]. A brief taxonomy was presented in this report, which compares silicon PUFs with the so-called non-silicon PUFs. Moreover, the authors of this research work examined evaluation criteria for PUFs as well as attacks on PUFs and the related countermeasures. The applications of PUFs were covered as well. A trend analysis on ring oscillator PUFs was the last subject addressed in this review. The state of the art in SRAM PUFs was discussed [126] along with some results from using them in the real-world industry. This report evaluated the entropy and the randomness provided by this kind of PUFs. Moreover, the limitations in the application of SRAM PUFs as well as the related design objectives were examined in this report.

A tutorial on PUFs and their applications was presented in [130]. This tutorial highlighted strong PUFs as promising mechanisms for authentication, and weak PUFs as proper solutions for key generation. In this report, trends in implementation technologies and emerging concepts in this area were discussed as well. The authors of [258] reviewed lightweight PUFs. They studied the design paradigms as well as the implementation methods and issues of lightweight PUFs, and examined their security.

2015: A taxonomy on PUFs with a special focus on configurability was presented in [290]. The author studied the requirements and proposed a novel reconfigurable ring oscillator PUF after the review. Helper data algorithms used in PUFs were reviewed and analyzed in [81], which led to the identification of some related threats as well as the introduction of some open problems in this area. A reliability model for PUFs was introduced and analyzed in this report. Moreover, some post-processes such as entropy compression, error correction and bit selection were examined in this research. A method for classifying PUFs and their security objectives was introduced in [278]. This classification method was based on a novel definition for PUF and some proposed classification criteria. This report provided topics for future research on PUFs. An overview on the applications of strong PUFs in lightweight authentication systems was presented in [82]. The authors of this report studied the relevant research studies in a chronological order to show the evolution of these applications. They studied the requirements of the applications and how strong PUFs fulfill these requirements.

2016: Different technologies used in the implementation of PUFs were compared in [16] in terms of CMOS synthesizability, randomness, uniqueness, scalability, reproducibility and area. The authors of this report specifically focused on emerging technologies. A review on silicon PUFs was presented in [267]. At the end of the review, a novel silicon PUF was proposed by the authors. PUFs based on nanotechnology were studied in [110]. The authors started with a review on traditional PUFs, performance metrics and applications. They continued with nanoelectronics-based PUFs and the related challenges and opportunities.

2017: The authors of [306] reviewed hybrid CMOS-resistive random number generators and PUFs based on SST (spin transfer torque)-DRAMs, metal-oxide RAMs and NVM (non-volatile memory) devices.

2018: A survey on DRAM-based TRNGs (true random number generators) and PUFs and their applications was presented in [26]. This report studied security metrics for these primitives as well as existing attacks on them. In this report, the two aforementioned primitives were compared with other hardware security primitives. Moreover, the history of PUFs was briefly reviewed in this research. Different types of PUFs and their applications in hardware security were studied in [89]. In this research, different design objectives for PUFs were studied.

2019: A literature review on PUFs was presented in [25] aiming at simple explanations for absolutely new researches in this area. This report covers related security threats and attacks. Applications of PUFs in Internet of things (IoT) were reviewed in [33]. This report investigated the treats in IoT systems that suggest the application of PUFs along with the related defense strategy. After a brief classification of PUFs, the corresponding protocols for IoT were studied.

Results from a survey on the applications of PUF in key management and authentication in IoT systems were presented in [323]. In this review, security challenges in IoT-based systems as well as well-known attacks on these systems were studied. Then, hardware-based security objectives were investigated, and PUF was introduced with a focus on SRAM-based and ReRAM (resistive RAM)-based PUFs. In the next step, fuzzy extractors and their applications in key generation were studied. The authors of [231] argued that some types of PUFs have received a research focus, while some other promising types have been overshadowed. They presented a taxonomy on PUFs, which aims at alleviating this problem. They established novel links between different types of PUFs on the basis of the underpinning physical mechanisms. They classified PUFs according to the source of randomness, the applications and families. They analyzed the taxonomy to identify types of PUF that need more attention from researchers. A very brief survey on PUFs was presented in [307]. Moreover, arbiter PUFs and their applications in device authentication were reviewed in [184].

Table 4.1 compares existing surveys and reviews on PUFs. The first three columns in Table 4.1 show the order of each survey in a chronological sorting, the research report presenting the survey and the related year of publication, respectively. The fourth column shows the number of research reports studied in the survey. The fifth column indicates whether the survey covers the general concept of PUF in all of its aspects or focuses on a specific type/application. The sixth, the seventh and the eighth columns indicate the existence or the lack of evolution study, trend analysis and future roadmap, respectively. Finally, the ninth column indicates whether or not the survey takes a statistical approach.

4.2 MOTIVATIONS

Table 4.1 states the following important points regarding the existing surveys:

1. Some of the existing surveys are too old for an increasingly growing field such as PUFs. The trend analyses, taxonomies and future roadmaps presented in these surveys can no longer be considered dependable. As an example, our sample space contains 125, 64, 504 PUF-related research works published before, during and after 2014. Thus, if a survey published in 2014 covers all papers published before its own publication year and half of the papers published during the same year, it can cover only 23 percent of our sample papers.

2. Some surveys do not study all aspects of PUFs such as components, types, design objectives and applications. They are confined to some specific kinds or applications of PUFs.

#	RP	Y	NR	G	E	T	F	S
1	[90]	2010	29	-	-	-	-	-
2	[220]	2010	58	✓	-	-	✓	-
3	[360]	2012	?	✓	-	-	-	-
4	[303]	2012	134	✓	✓	-	-	-
5	[304]	2014	82	✓	-	-	-	-
6	[305]	2014	51	-	-	-	✓	-
7	[389]	2014	99	-	-	✓	-	-
8	[126]	2014	-	-	-			-
9	[130]	2014	42	✓	-	✓	-	-
10	[258]	2014	27	-	-	-	-	-
11	[290]	2015	29	✓	-	-	✓	-
12	[81]	2015	47	-	-	-	-	-
13	[278]	2015	19	✓	-	-	✓	-
14	[82]	2015	61	✓	-	-	✓	-
15	[16]	2016	26	✓	✓	-	-	-
16	[267]	2016	15	-	-	-	-	-
17	[110]	2016	99	-	-	-	-	-
18	[306]	2017	95	-	-	-	-	-
19	[26]	2018	98	-	✓	-	-	-
20	[89]	2018	9	-	-	-	-	-
21	[25]	2019	13	✓	-	-	-	-
22	[33]	2019	84	-	-	-	-	-
23	[323]	2019	191	-	-	-	-	-
24	[231]	2019	103	✓	-	-	✓	-
25	[307]	2019	10	✓	-	-	-	-
26	[184]	2019	29	-	-	-	-	-

Table 4.1 A Summary of Existing Surveys

3. While a proper evolution study can help researchers reach a better understanding of research on PUFs, and further can clarify existing trends, only a small fraction of existing surveys present such a study.

4. Some surveys fail to highlight existing trends or outline topics for future research.

5. Existing surveys generally study a limited number of research reports, which makes it difficult to introduce and analyze

existing trends with certainty. For example, the average number of references in the 6 surveys published in 2019 is less than 72, while in our samples 133 research reports regarding PUFs have been published only in 2018. In fact, the lack of a systematic and automatic analysis approach makes it unfeasible to study a large-enough sample space of research reports.

The aforementioned shortcomings motivate us to study a large set of research reports systematically in order to present an evolution study and a trend analysis on PUFs as well as a roadmap for future research on this topic.

4.3 METHODOLOGY

Our trend analysis methodology depends on a text-mining tool and statistical engine. The text-mining tool consists of three components: a lexer, a classifier and a robot. The statistical engine consists of four components: a historical analysis, a recent year analysis, a top journal analysis and a top conference analysis. The process and the role of the components can be explained in the following steps.

1. In the preprocess phase, a lexer extracts 1020 keywords from the titles of 577 PUF-related research reports (primary reports) randomly chosen from the "Google" search engine and the "IEEE Xplore" database. The lexer uses some simple rule set for cleanup and tokenization. For example, the cleanup procedure removes prepositions, articles and punctuation characters. Moreover, the tokenization procedure identifies compositions connected by "-" or "/". The latter procedure joins the words "based", "code" and "detection" to their previous words and words such as numbers, "multiple" or "bit" to their next words. The rule sets have been modified in a few iterations.

2. A semi-automatic classification has been applied to the keywords to make 295 meaningful research topics out of them. Part of the classification process is performed by an automatic classifier. For example, keywords differing only in lower/upper case are in the same class, and words with a suffix/prefix relation are joined to make a single class. Moreover, words ending at related suffixes such as "ance" and "ant" or "able" and "ability" are automatically joined to

form a single class. But part of the classification needs to be performed manually due to the existence of complicated semantic, discourse and pragmatic relations. For example, there are some complex compositions such as "Spin Transfer Switching Characteristics". As another example, the word "aging" should be considered in the context as the aging effect is used for building PUFs in some research works, and considered as undesired environmental effect in others. The output of the classification is a corpus containing 295 topics. The corpus is used to form a classification tree, which represents the final classification of the topics. The classification tree consists of two types of nodes. Some nodes directly correspond to topics in the corpus. These nodes are referred to as topic nodes. A second group of nodes have been added to connect topics to each other. The latter nodes are called class nodes. In Figures 5.2 through 5.21 (except for Figure 5.19), blue boxes represent topic nodes, and class nodes are represented by light brown boxes.

3. A set of 116 secondary reports are added to the primary ones, and the robot tool works on the entire set of reports after being trained by the corpus. The robot tool searches for each key word of each topic in the title of each research report.

4. The matches reported by the robot tool are fed into the statistical engine for four types of analyses. The historical analysis calculates the popularity of each topic since 2002 (when the term "PUF" was coined) up to 2019, and identifies the most frequent and the most cited topics during this period of time. The recent years' analyses identify the most frequent and the most cited topics that have appeared in research reports published in recent years (2017-2019). The top conference and journal analyses identify the most frequent and the most cited topics that have appeared in top conferences and journals. Top conferences or journals are the ones that have published the largest number of papers or the most cited papers regarding PUF.

5. After identifying the most popular topics, the variations of their popularity are analyzed during the course of time to identify the trends. The outcome of the statistical engine is

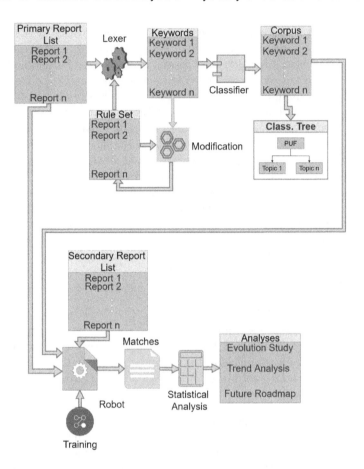

Figure 4.1 The Trend Analysis Methodology: The text-mining tool scans the whole sample space after being trained and building the corpus. It suggests topics to be analyzed by the statistical engine.

used for evolution study and future roadmap development, as well.

Figure 4.1 shows the research methodology used in this book.

4.4 WORK SPACE

The work space of the text-mining tool consists of two sets of research reports. A set of 577 primary research reports have been used in the training phase and another set of 116 secondary reports have been used (in addition to the primary ones) in the statistical analysis phase. Those reports that have been cited in the text are included in the bibliography at the end of this book. But others that have been used only by the text-mining tool are included in the e-resource. See Table 4.2 for the details.

| | | Cited or Not Cited in the Text ||
		Cited in the Text	Not Cited (E-Resource)
Category	Primary	[1-2], [6-12], [15-20], [22-37], [39-41], [43-46], [47-53], [393]	[1-528]
	Secondary	[14], [21], [42], [292]	[529-640]

Table 4.2 The Work Space of the Text-Mining Tool

CHAPTER 5

The Classification Tree and Popularities

In this chapter, we introduce the classification tree. In order to make the figures more manageable, we have broken the tree into several parts shown in Figures 5.2 through 5.18, 5.20 and 5.21. Below each node in the tree, two numbers can be seen. The one on the left side shows the number of research reports related to the topic or the class, and the one on the right shows the number of citations to the related research reports. For a class node, these numbers are simply the sum of the corresponding numbers in the subtree. But for topic nodes, the numbers of the topic are added to the sum. Citation numbers have been checked in scientific databases such as IEEExplore and Google Scholar. For reports indexed in more than one database, the maximum citation number has been considered.

5.1   FIRST-LEVEL CLASSIFICATION AND LIFE CYCLE

The first-level classification of the topics suggested by the text-mining tool can be inspired by the phases in the life cycle of PUF. To the best of our knowledge, there is no research report or standard focusing on the development of a life cycle for PUFs. Thus, we consider the hypothetical life cycle shown in Figure 5.1.

According to the life cycle shown in Figure 5.1, the first level of the classification tree is built as shown in Figure 5.2.

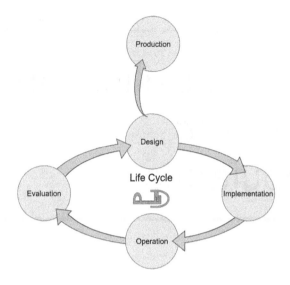

Figure 5.1 PUF Life Cycle.

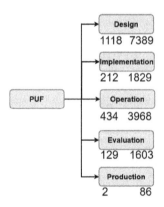

Figure 5.2 First-Level Classification of Topics.

All the nodes in Figure 5.2 are class nodes. This figure illustrates that, based on our classification, the topics related to the Design phase have been more popular than those of the other phases. Furthermore, Figure 5.2 clearly shows that the Evaluation phase and the Production phase need to be addressed further. Another interesting comparison between the Design phase and the

Implementation phase is that although topics related to the Design phase are shown to be more popular, the average number of citations is larger for the Implementation phase.

5.2 DESIGN

In this section, we study the design-related topics, their popularities and the corresponding classification subtrees. The subtree of the Design node in Figure 5.2 can be broken to smaller subtrees, as shown in Figure 5.3. The subtree of each individual leaf node in Figure 5.3 will be studied separately in the following sections.

In Figure 5.3, the class expansion contains the topics related to the expansion from stand-alone PUFs to interconnected PUFs.

As shown in Figure 5.3, Design Objectives and Component Design classes are relatively popular, while the others (especially Standardization) have not been studied adequately. However, the average number of citations is notable for Modeling and Alternatives topics. According to this figure, the tradeoffs between design objectives apparently need to be investigated.

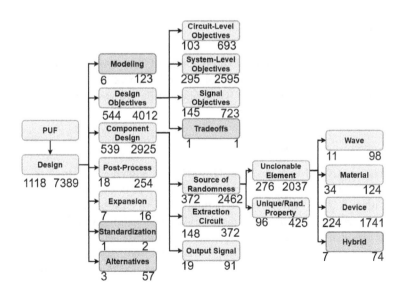

Figure 5.3 The Subtree of "Design" Broken into Smaller Subtrees.

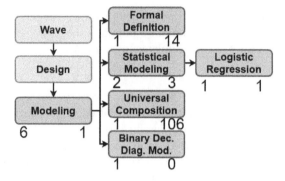

Figure 5.4 The Subtree of "Modeling".

5.2.1 Modeling

Figure 5.4 shows the subtree of the Modeling node.

Figure 5.4 highlights a need for more research on formal definitions for PUFs.

5.2.2 Design Objectives

As shown in Figure 5.3, the node Design Objectives has four subtrees with roots at Circuit-Level Objectives, System-Level Objectives, Signal Objectives and Tradeoffs. These subtrees are discussed in the following paragraphs.

System-Level Objectives

The subtree of System-Level Objectives is shown in Figure 5.5.

The width, the depth and the number of nodes in the subtree of Figure 5.5 indicate the overall popularity of System-Level Objectives. However, a need for more research focus on Fault-Tolerance is primarily seen at first glance. Furthermore, the deepest branch in this subtree ends at leaf topic nodes related to noise immunity, which can be considered as an indicator of the depth of research in this branch.

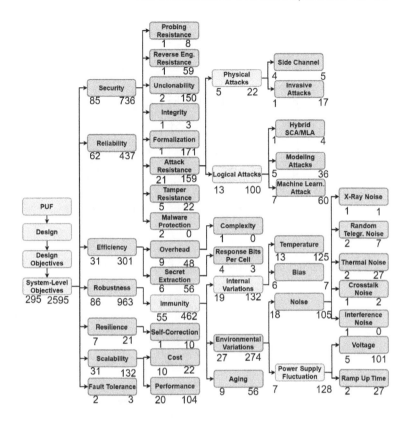

Figure 5.5 The Subtree of "System-Level Objectives".

Circuit-Level Objectives

The subtree of the Design-Level Objectives class node can be seen in Figure 5.6.

After the popularity-related numbers, the most important point regarding the subtree in Figure 5.6 is its depth, width and number of nodes being less than those of the subtree of System-Level Objectives.

Signal Objectives and Tradeoffs

Figure 5.7 shows the subtree of Signal Objectives along with that of Tradeoffs (which is empty).

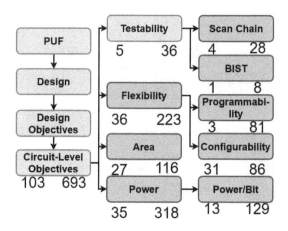

Figure 5.6 The Subtree of "Circuit-Level Objectives".

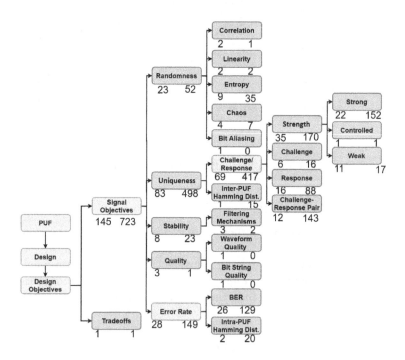

Figure 5.7 The Subtrees of "Signal Objectives" and "Tradeoffs".

The deepest branch in the subtree of Figure 5.7 is the one ending at topics corresponding to the strength of PUFs. The popularity of topics BER (Bit Error Rate), Strong (strong PUF) and Challenge-Response Pair is worth noting in this subtree. Moreover, one may observe the high average number of citations for the topic Intra-PUF Hamming Distance.

5.2.3 Component Design

It can be seen in Figure 5.3 that Design Components have three subtrees, the roots of which are Source of Randomness, Extraction Circuit and Output signal.

Source of Randomness

This class has two subtrees discussed below.

1. Unclonable Element: This class node has the following four subtrees.

    (a) Wave

    (b) Material

    (c) Device

    (d) Hybrid

2. Unique/Random Property

    The subtrees of Wave and Material are shown in Figure 5.8.

    An interesting comparison can be made between Wave and Material in Figure 5.8. Although Material is more popular, the average number of citations is higher for Wave.

    Figure 5.9 shows the subtrees of Device and Hybrid.

    As seen in Figure 5.9, width, depth and the number of nodes in the subtree Device are substantially higher than those of Wave, Material and Hybrid. Although the figure indicates that Memories is very popular, the average number of citations is larger for Latch-Based Circuits. This figure highlights a notable difference between the popularities of Volatile Memory and Non-Volatile Memory. Another interesting observation is the high average number of citations for D Flip-Flop.

    The subtree of Variable Property can be seen in Figure 5.10

    The popularity of Delay can be clearly seen in Figure 5.10. The high number of citations for Aging Effect and the high average

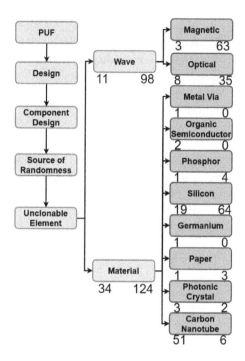

Figure 5.8 The Subtrees of "Wave" and "Material".

number of citations for Geometry and Write Time are notable in this figure.

Extraction Circuit and Output Signal

Figure 5.11 demonstrates the subtrees of Extraction Circuit and Output Signal.

Figure 5.11 highlights the popularity of Ring Oscillator and Arbiter.

5.2.4 Post-Process, Expansion, Standardization and Alternatives

The subtrees of Post-Process, Expansion, Standardization and Alternatives are shown in Figure 5.12.

Figure 5.12 shows the popularity of Helper Data Algorithm and Error Correction.

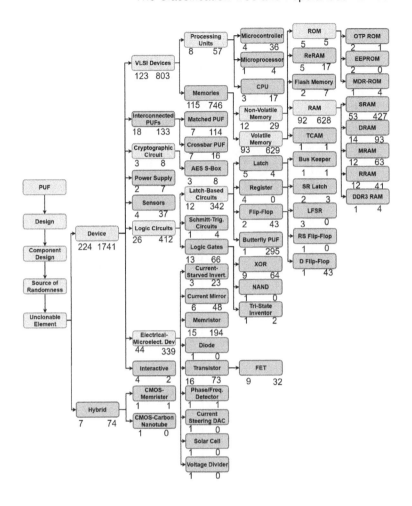

Figure 5.9 The Subtrees of "Device" and "Hybrid".

5.3 IMPLEMENTATION

The subtree of Implementation can be seen in Figure 5.13.

The high popularities of FPGA and CMOS are clearly seen in Figure 5.13. The high average number of citations for ASIC is another point to note in this figure.

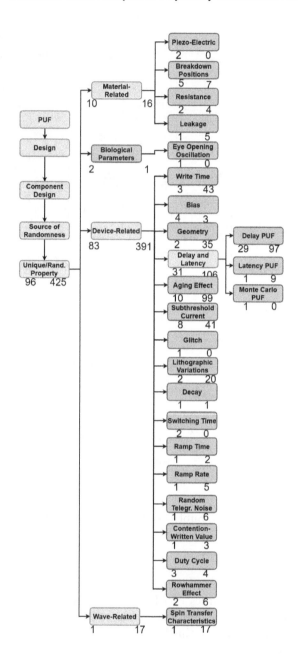

Figure 5.10 The Subtree of "Variable Property".

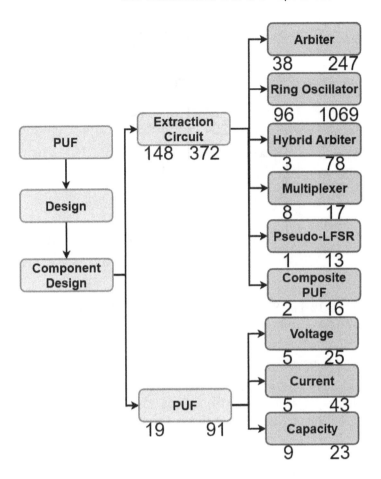

Figure 5.11 The Subtrees of "Extraction Circuit" and "Output Signal".

5.4 OPERATION

The subtree of Operation can be broken into smaller subtrees, as shown in Figure 5.14.

Each leaf node in Figure 5.14 has a subtree. These subtrees are discussed in the following.

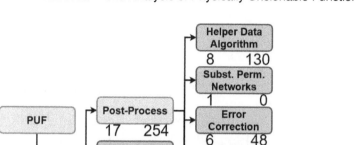

Figure 5.12 The Subtrees of "Post-Process", "Expansion", "Standardization" and "Alternatives".

5.4.1 Ecosystem

As seen in Figure 5.14, Ecosystem has five subtrees: Enabling Technologies, Combined Mechanisms, Auxiliary Sciences, Auxiliary Techniques and Applications. These subtrees are discussed below.

Enabling Technologies and Combined Mechanisms

The subtrees of Enabling Technologies and Combined Mechanisms can be seen in Figure 5.15.

The most popular topics in Figure 5.15 are Fuzzy Systems and FSMs.

Auxiliary Sciences and Auxiliary Techniques

Figure 5.16 shows the subtrees of Auxiliary Sciences and Auxiliary Techniques. As seen in Figure 5.16, Pattern Recognition and Coding are more cited, while Reconfigurable Design is more frequent.

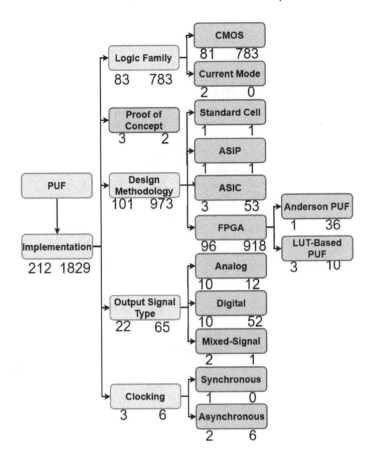

Figure 5.13 The Subtree of "Implementation".

Applications

As shown in Figure 5.14, Applications has the following two sub-trees.

1. Non-Security Applications

2. Security-Related Applications

Figure 5.17 shows the subtree of Non-Security Applications.

The high popularity of Resource-Constrained Systems, especially Embedded Systems, is clear from Figure 5.17. RFID is

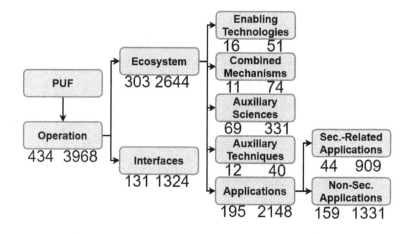

Figure 5.14 The Subtree of "Operation" Broken into Smaller Subtrees.

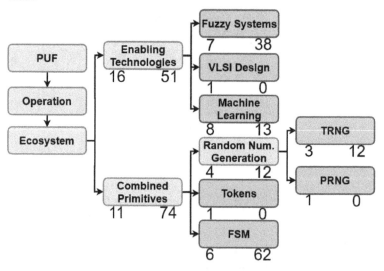

Figure 5.15 The Subtrees of "Enabling Technologies" and "Combined Mechanisms".

another highly popular topic that can be seen at a glance in this figure.

The subtree of Security Applications can be shown in Figure 5.18.

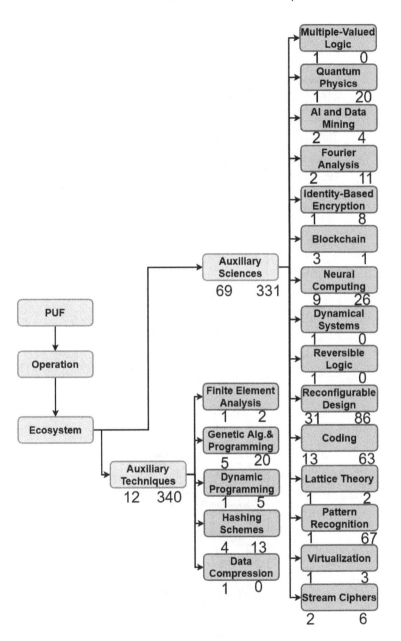

Figure 5.16 The Subtrees of "Auxiliary Sciences" and "Auxiliary Techniques".

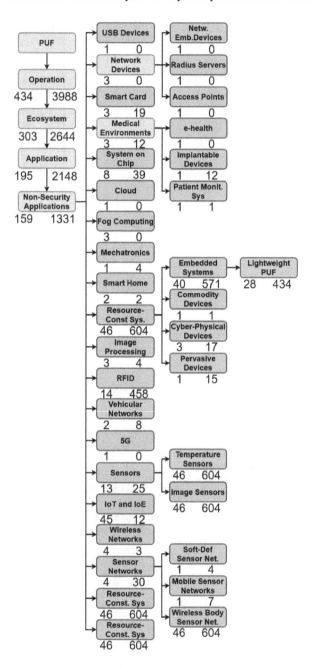

Figure 5.17 The Subtree of "Non-Security Applications".

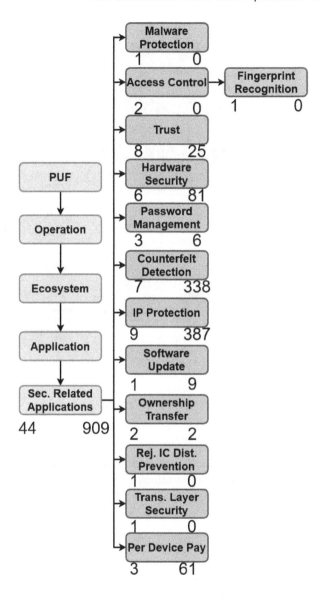

Figure 5.18 The Subtree of "Security Applications".

Figure 5.19 PUF Ecosystem.

The highly popular topics IP Protection and Counterfeit Detection are easily seen in Figure 5.18. However, one should note the high average number of citations for Per Device Pay as well.

Figure 5.19 shows the ecosystem of PUF as suggested by our text-mining tool.

5.4.2 Interfaces

The subtree of Interfaces is shown in Figure 5.20.

The most important information in Figure 5.20 is the high popularity of Authentication and Key Management. However, the high average number of citations for Public Key Encryption and Obfuscation should be noted, as well.

Figure 5.21 shows the subtrees of Evaluation and Production.

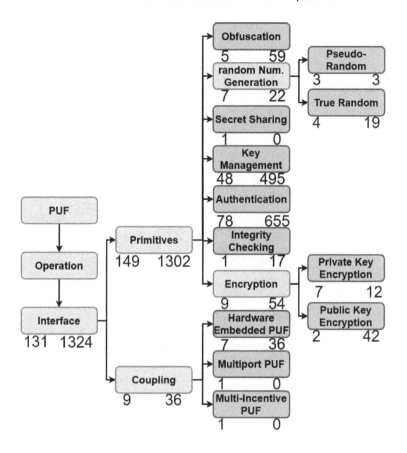

Figure 5.20 The Subtree of "Interfaces".

5.5 EVALUATION AND PRODUCTION

The first point to note in Figure 5.21 is the high popularity of Cloning, Modeling Attack and Machine Learning Attack. However, the high average number of citations for Cloning, Differential Template Attack and Cryptanalysis is another interesting point in this figure.

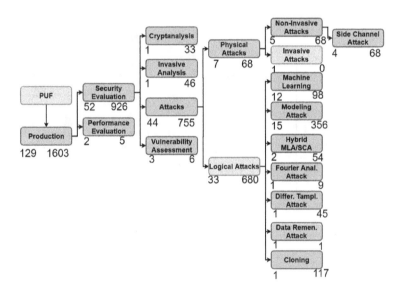

Figure 5.21 The Subtrees of "Evaluation" and "Production".

CHAPTER 6

Trend Analysis

In order to identify trends in research on PUF, one can take a traditional approach. For example, we can have a look at primitives presented by PUFs, different types of PUF, their applications, the related design considerations, etc. This way, we may identify several topics. Just to mention a few, we can refer to physical nanostructure-based PUFs [146, 352] or public PUFs [40, 302]. Moreover, we may notice their applications in sensors [295], virtual proofs of reality [299], oblivious transfer [298, 301] and universally composable secure computing [35, 47, 74, 266]. Another approach to trend identification can be based on the identification of highly cited research reports [121, 192, 203, 300] or the identification of the types of PUF that have several applications (such as strong PUFs [34, 72]). But this book aims at introducing a method that is systematic, based on well-defined topic popularity measures and as automatic as possible.

In this chapter, we first use the popularity statistics presented in Chapter 5 in order to identify the most popular topics to which we refer as top topics. Then, we analyze the variations of the popularity of each top topic during the course of time.

6.1 TOP TOPICS

In this section, we introduce the top topics. To do this, we present eight ranking tables that show the most frequent and the most cited topics during the history, in recent years, at top conferences and in top journals. The topics that appear in half or more of these tables are chosen as top topics.

6.1.1 The Most Popular Topics during the History

Table 6.1 shows the 10 most frequent topics during the history.

Number	Topic	Papers	Citations
1	Ring Oscillator	96	1069
2	FPGA	96	918
3	CMOS	81	783
4	Authentication	78	655
5	Evaluation	73	614
6	Reliability	62	437
7	SRAM	53	427
8	Security	51	641
9	Key Management	48	495
10	IoT	45	121

Table 6.1 The Most Frequent Topics during the History

The 10 most cited topics during the history are shown in Table 6.2.

Number	Topic	Papers	Citations
1	Ring Oscillator	96	1069
2	FPGA	96	918
3	CMOS	81	783
4	Authentication	78	655
5	Security	51	641
6	Evaluation	73	614
7	Robustness	31	503
8	Key Management.	48	495
9	RFID	14	458
10	Reliability	62	437

Table 6.2 The Most Cited Topics during the History

6.1.2   The Most Popular Topics in Top Conferences

In this subsection, we first outline the top conferences: the conferences that have published the largest numbers of PUF-related papers or the ones whose published papers have been most cited.

Conference Selection

In order to identify top conferences, we sorted 221 conferences that have published papers related to PUFs: first according to the number of papers, second according to the number of citations and third according to the average number of citations. After each sorting, we selected the top 10 in the sorted list. Then we merged the two to top 10 lists. The result is shown in Table 6.3.

The 19 conferences in Table 6.3 have published 220 papers regarding PUFs.

Topic Selection

179 out of 295 topics have been studied in top conferences. We have sorted these topics according to the number of papers as well as the number of citations. Table 6.4 shows the 10 most frequent topics that appeared in top conferences.

The 10 most cited topics that appeared in top conferences are listed in Table 6.5.

6.1.3   Popular Topics in Top Journals

In this subsection, we introduce the most popular topics that appeared in papers published by top journals. The top journals and the corresponding most popular topics have been identified through a process similar to the case of top conferences.

Journal Selection

The top journals listed in Table 6.6 have been selected from 53 journals that have published PUF-related papers.

Topic Selection

The journals listed in Table 6.6 have published 90 papers regarding PUFs, and 123 out of 295 topics have appeared in these papers.

Conference	#P	#C	AvC
IEEE International Symposium on Hardware Oriented Security and Trust (HOST)	44	1088	24.73
IEEE International Symposium on Circuits and Systems (ISCAS)	43	131	3.05
Design, Automation & Test in Europe Conference & Exhibition (DATE)	35	335	9.57
IEEE Computer Society Annual Symposium on VLSI	19	63	3.32
ACM/IEEE Design Automation Conference (DAC)	15	111	7.4
IEEE International Midwest Symposium on Circuits and Systems (MWSCAS)	13	6	0.5
Euromicro Conference on Digital System Design	11	86	7.82
IEEE/ACM International Conference on Computer-Aided Design (ICCAD)	9	348	38.7
Asia and South Pacific Design Automation Conference	9	141	15.67
International Symposium on Quality Electronic Design (ISQED)	9	39	4.33
IEEE International Workshop on Hardware-Oriented Security and Trust	2	336	168
IEEE International Conference on RFID	5	314	62.8
International Workshop on Information Forensics and Security (WIFS)	3	164	54.67
IEEE International Solid-State Circuits Conference (ISSCC)	8	155	19.38
IEEE European Symposium on Security and Privacy Workshops (EuroS&PW)	3	149	49.7
Annual Cryptology Conference (Crypto)	1	106	106
International Conference on Information Security	1	69	69
IEEE Symposium on Security and Privacy Workshops	1	59	59
International Conference on Network and System Security	1	26	26

TABLE 6.3 Top Conferences

Number	Topic	Papers	Citations
1	CMOS	34	278
2	Authentication	31	351
3	FPGA	23	200
4	Key Management	21	353
5	Reliability	21	195
6	Security	20	131
7	Ring Oscillator	16	177
8	IoT	16	81
9	Evaluation	15	103
10	Area	13	49

Table 6.4 The Most Frequent Topics in Top Conferences

Number	Topic	Papers	Citations
1	Key Management	21	353
2	Authentication	31	351
3	Lightweight PUF	9	337
4	CMOS	34	278
5	RFID	3	259
6	FPGA	23	200
7	Modeling Attack	3	198
8	Reliability	21	195
9	Ring Oscillator	16	177
10	Robustness	11	160

Table 6.5 The Most Cited Topics in Top Conferences

The most frequent topics in the aforementioned papers are the ones listed in Table 6.7.

Table 6.8 contains the most cited topics in top journals.

6.1.4 Popular Topics in Recent Years

In this subsection, we introduce the most popular topics in recent years (2017, 2018 and 2019). We have sorted 205 out of 295 topics studied in recent years according to the number of papers as well as the number of citations. The most frequent recent topics are shown in Table 6.9.

Journal	#P	#C	AvC
IEEE Transactions on Information Forensics and Security	16	451	28.19
IEEE Transactions on Circuits and Systems	14	95	6.79
IEEE Transactions on Computer-Aided Design of Integrated Circuits and Systems	11	302	27.45
IEEE Journal of Solid-State Circuits	9	43	4.78
IEEE Transactions on Very Large Scale Integration (VLSI) Systems	7	37	5.29
IEEE Transactions on Emerging Topics in Computing	6	155	28.83
Electronics Letters	6	65	10.83
IEEE Transactions on Multi-Scale Computing Systems	4	51	12.75
IEEE Solid-State Circuits Letters	4	8	2
IEEE Transactions on Computers	4	1	0.25
IEEE Journal on Emerging and Selected Topics in Circuits and Systems	1	52	52
IEEE Transactions on Nanotechnology	3	36	12
Advanced Functional Materials	1	30	30
International Journal of Quantum Information	1	20	20
Journal of Information Processing	1	18	18
IEEE Transactions on Magnetics	1	17	17
IEEE Design & Test	2	33	16.5
IEEE Transactions on Information Theory	1	15	15

TABLE 6.6   Top Journals

Table 6.10 lists the most cited recent topics.

Tables 6.1, 6.2, 6.4, 6.5, 6.7, 6.8, 6.9 and 6.10 contain 22 different topics. Among these topics, nine top topics have appeared in half or more of the tables. Figure 6.1 shows the nine top topics and their locations in the classification tree.

Number	Topic	Papers	Citations
1	CMOS	17	118
2	Authentication	12	51
3	Reliability	11	57
4	Security	10	59
5	Ring Oscillator	9	158
6	FPGA	7	19
7	Evaluation	6	55
8	Area	6	35
9	Key Management	6	25
10	IoT	6	20

Table 6.7 The Most Frequent Topics in Top Journals

Number	Topic	Papers	Citations
1	Ring Oscillator	9	158
2	CMOS	17	118
3	Power	5	81
4	Magnetic	3	63
5	Arbiter	3	60
6	Security	10	59
7	Reliability	11	57
8	Evaluation	6	55
9	Lightweight PUF	5	55
10	Memristor	3	52

Table 6.8 Most Cited Topics in Top Journals

Number	Topic	Papers	Citations
1	CMOS	44	64
2	FPGA	37	125
3	IoT	37	48
4	Authentication	36	95
5	Reliability	35	103
6	Ring Oscillator	34	98
7	SRAM	31	55
8	Evaluation	27	28
9	Key Management	21	63
10	Arbiter	21	22

Table 6.9 Most Frequent Topics in Recent Years

Number	Topic	Papers	Citations
1	FPGA	37	125
2	Reliability	35	103
3	Ring Oscillator	34	98
4	Authentication	36	95
5	Programmability	1	70
6	BER	17	65
7	CMOS	9	64
8	XOR	44	64
9	Key Management	21	63
10	SRAM	10	60

Table 6.10 Most Cited Topics in Recent Years

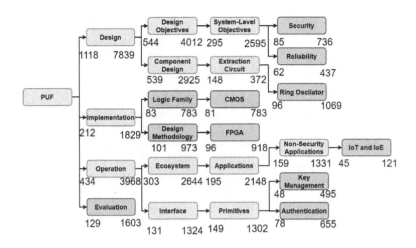

Figure 6.1 Top Topics in the Classification Tree.

6.2 EVOLUTION STUDY

In this section, we study the evolution of PUFs via highlighting the topics that have appeared in research reports for the first time each year. The term "Physical Unclonable Function" has been coined for the first time in 2002 [113]. The first PUF-related research in our list (consisting of 693 reports) has been published in 2003 [185]. Then there is no report in this area before 2007 (it is not far from the reality, because the research community might have needed time to internalize the notion of PUF). Thus, our evolution study starts in 2007. Figure 6.2 shows the results of our evolution study.

Figure 6.2 The Evolution of PUF.

Future Roadmap

In this chapter, we outline some topics for future research in the area of PUF (Figure 7.1) on the basis of two different strategies explained below.

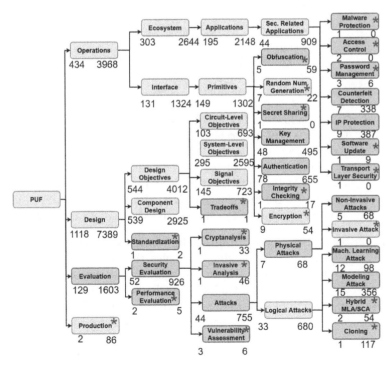

Figure 7.1 Topics for Future Research on PUF.

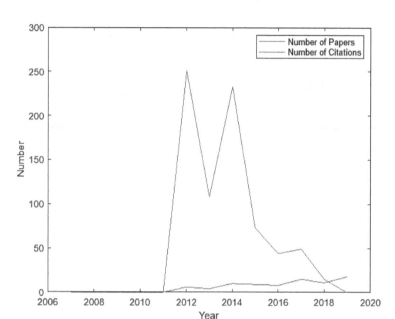

Figure 7.2 The Popularity of "CMOS".

Figure 7.2 shows the popularity curves of CMOS.

1. Trend Following: The idea behind this strategy is to work on the topics expected to be popular in the future. In fact, this is the strategy that has led to the saturation in the popularity of some top topics in recent years, as explained in Section 7.1. Researchers interested in this strategy are recommended to conduct research on IoT, Key Management and FPGA, although this strategy can lead to saturation in near future.

2. Scope Broadening: This strategy suggests widening the research area via working on topics that have received less attention so far, which would lead to new top topics. The classification tree introduced in Chapter 5 makes it possible to select topics on the basis of this strategy. To do this, we simply select the strategic topic or class nodes that are considerably less popular than their siblings at this point (in terms of the number of papers and/or the number of citations). These nodes are marked by red asterisks in Figure 7.1.

7.1 TRENDS

We studied the popularities of all 295 topics in Chapter 5. In this section, we further elaborate on top topics introduced in Section 6.1 via analyzing the variations of the popularity of each of them during the evolution of PUFs.

The blue curve in Figure 7.2 shows the variations of the number of reports, and the red one shows the number of citations. We refer to the mentioned curves as the reports curve and the citations curve, respectively. The last peak in the citations curve appears in 2017. The two curves cross in 2019. This shows a decrease in the number of citations despite the increase in the number of reports. Part of the decrease can be justified by the rationale that reports published in recent years need time to be cited. But one may note that there are reports with more than 50 citations published in 2019 [386]. Thus, the cross between the curves suggests a sign of saturation in the popularity of the topic CMOS in terms of citations. Figure 7.3 shows the popularity curves for Reliability.

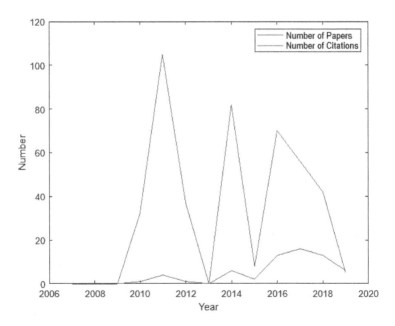

Figure 7.3 The Popularity of "Reliability".

Both the curves in Figure 7.3 show a descending trajectory in recent years. This should be considered as a sign of gradual loss of popularity for the topic Reliability.

The popularity diagram of Ring Oscillator can be seen in Figure 7.4.

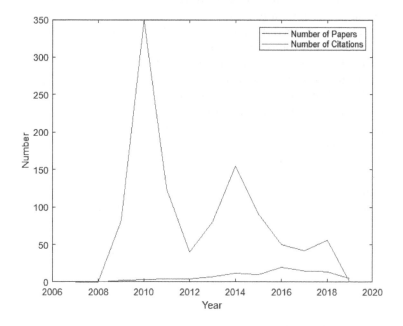

Figure 7.4 The Popularity of "Ring Oscillator".

A recent peak in the citations curve of Ring Oscillator shown in Figure 7.4 is to some extent overshadowed by the descending trend of the reports curve.

The curves in Figure 7.5 show the popularity of Authentication.

As seen in Figure 7.5, the last peak in the citations curve for Authentication appears in 2015. Given the low average height of the reports curve and its flat trend in recent years, the overall popularity of Authentication should be considered descending.

The popularity curves of FPGA are shown in Figure 7.6.

Figure 7.6 shows a recent ascending trend in the citations curve of FPGA. A slightly descending trend in the reports curve is not significant enough to overshadow the increasing number of citations. Thus, FPGA is not predicted to lose its popularity in the next few years.

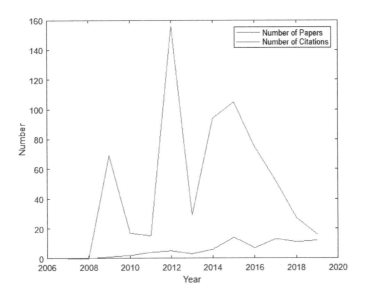

Figure 7.5 The Popularity of "Authentication".

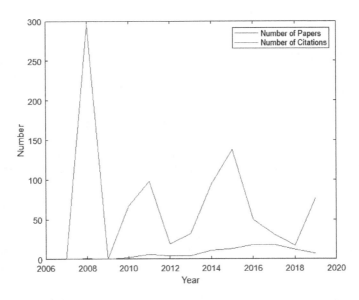

Figure 7.6 The Popularity of "FPGA".

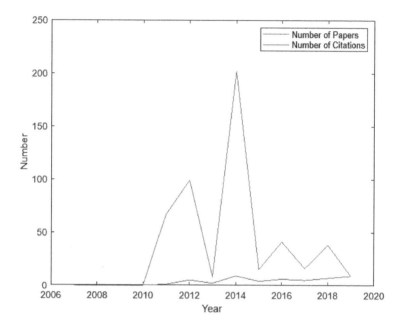

Figure 7.7 The Popularity of "Key Management".

Figure 7.7 shows the popularity diagram for Key Management.

According to Figure 7.7, two bouncing citations curve of Key Management as well as its somewhat flat reports curve are predicted to keep their trends in the next few years.

Popularity curves of Security are shown in Figure 7.8.

The citations curve and the reports curve of Security cross in 2108, as shown in Figure 7.8. An analysis similar to the case of CMOS predicts Security to gradually lose its popularity in the forthcoming years.

Figure 7.9 shows the variations of the number of reports and the number of citations of IoT.

Figure 7.9 predicts the popularity of IoT to increase or at least remain stable in the next few years. There are some reasons behind this prediction. First, the peaks in the curves of IoT are more recent than those of the other topics. Second, the curves have not gone below the average, although they have been slightly descending in 2019.

Finally, the variations in the popularity of Evaluation are shown in Figure 7.10.

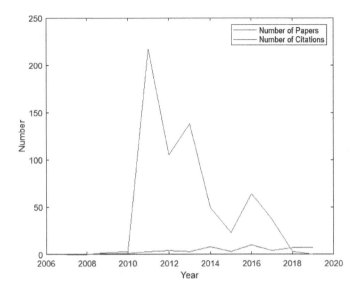

Figure 7.8 The Popularity of "Security".

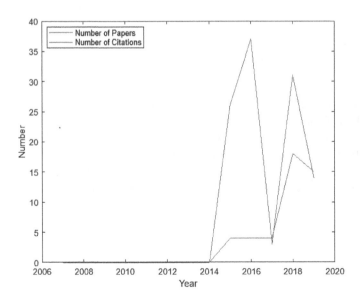

Figure 7.9 The Popularity of "IoT".

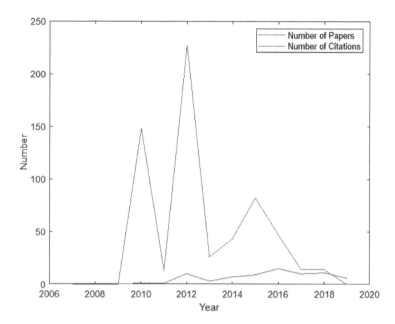

Figure 7.10 The Popularity of "Evaluation".

According to Figure 7.10 and via an analysis similar to those presented for CMOS and Security, Evaluation is predicted to gradually decline in popularity in the forthcoming years.

The reports curves and the citations curves of all top topics have been brought together in Figures 7.11 and 7.12 in order to allow a comparison among them.

Figure 7.11 suggests IoT and Key Management as the most promising topics for the next few years.

Figure 7.12 clearly highlights FPGA as the only topic with a considerably increasing trend in recent years.

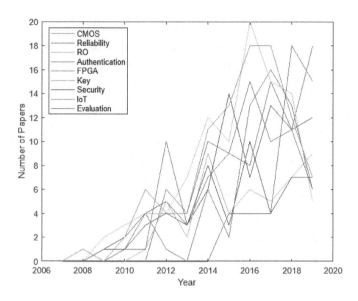

Figure 7.11 Top Topics: Number of Papers.

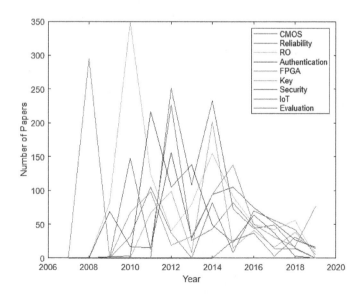

Figure 7.12 Top Topics: Number of Citations.

7.2 CONCLUSIONS AND FURTHER WORK

In this book, we have demonstrated that the popularity of PUF in the research community has been following a decreasing trend in recent years. We suggested future roadmaps based on evolution study and trend analysis as a solution to this problem. We showed that existing surveys in this area fail to study an adequate number of research reports due to their non-systematic approaches. We then systematically analyzed the popularities of PUF-related research topics deduced by a text-mining tool. Our systematic statistical analyses lead to the identification of nine popular topics, of which six topics are not expected to keep their popularities in the near future. We presented a future roadmap focusing on less studied aspects of PUF, which can help keep PUF popular in the future. Our work in this book can be continued by research on the topics presented in the future roadmap.

Bibliography

[1] Altera reveals stratix 10 with intrinsic-id's PUF technology. https://www.intrinsic-id.com/altera-reveals-stratix-10-with-intrinsic-ids-puf-technology/. Accessed: 2020-08-07.

[2] Physical unclonable function. https://www.intrinsic-id.com/sram-puf/. Accessed: 2020-08-07.

[3] Physical unclonable functions. https://www.ei.tum.de/en/sec/research/physical-unclonable-functions/. Accessed: 2020-08-20.

[4] Physical unclonable functions and applications. http://people.csail.mit.edu/rudolph/Teaching/Lectures/Security/Lecture-Security-PUFs-2.pdf. Accessed: 2020-08-08.

[5] Physical unclonable functions (PUF) basics. https://www.coursera.org/lecture/hardware-security/physical-unclonable-functions-puf-basics-Ab4sf. Accessed: 2020-08-07.

[6] Physically unclonable function-based password generation scheme. https://nau.edu/nau-research/available-technologies/cybersecurity-innovations/unclonable-function/. Accessed: 2020-08-07.

[7] Physically unclonable function database (PUFdb). http://www.green-ic.org/pufdb. Accessed: 2020-08-07.

[8] Physically unclonable function (PUF) solution for ARC EM processors. https://www.synopsys.com/dw/doc.php/ds/cc/intrinsic-ID_PUF_ARC_EM.pdf. Accessed: 2020-08-07.

[9] Research projects. https://caslab.csl.yale.edu/research.html. Accessed: 2020-08-07.

[10] TMD - optical physical unclonable functions (PUFs) for device authentication. https://med.nyu.edu/oil/industry/technologies-licensing/devices/tmd-optical-physical-unclonable-functionspufs-device-authentication. Accessed: 2020-08-07.

[11] Xilinx addresses rigorous security demands at fifth annual working group for broad range of applications. https://www.prnewswire.com/news-releases/xilinx-addresses-rigorous-security-demands-at-fifth-annual-working-group-for-broad-range-of-applications-300351291.html. Accessed: 2020-08-07.

[12] In *Proceedings of*, Bandung, Indonesia, July 2019. https://www.worldscientific.com/doi/abs/10.1142/S0218126618501384

[13] Mark D. Aagaard, Guang Gong, and Rajesh K. Mota. Hardware implementations of the WG-5 cipher for passive rfid tags. In *Proceedings of IEEE International Symposium on Hardware-Oriented Security and Trust (HOST)*, Austin, TX, USA, June 2013.

[14] Mohamed M. Abdel-Aziz and Amr T. Abdel-Hamid. Hardware low power implementation of attribute-based encryption. In *Proceedings of 28th International Conference on Microelectronics (ICM)*, Giza, Egypt, December 2016.

[15] Abubakr Abdulgadir, William Diehl, and Jens-Peter Kaps. An open-source platform for evaluation of hardware implementations of lightweight authenticated ciphers. In *Proceedings of International Conference on ReConFigurable Computing and FPGAs (ReConFig)*, Cancun, Mexico, December 2019.

[16] Ilia A. Bautista Adames, Jayita Das, and Sanjukta Bhanja. Survey of emerging technology based physical unclonable functions. In *Proceedings of International Great Lakes Symposium on VLSI (GLSVLSI)*, Boston, MA, USA, May 2016.

[17] T. Addabbo, M. Di Marco, A. Fort, M. Mugnaini, H. Takaloo, and V. Vignoli. A CMOS PUF circuit primitive based on a two-dimensional nonlinear dynamical system. In *Proceedings of IEEE International Symposium on Circuits and Systems (ISCAS)*, Sapporo, Japan, May 2019.

[18] Anita Aghaie, Mehran Mozaffari Kermani, and Reza Azarderakhsh. Reliable and fault diagnosis architectures for hardware and software-efficient block cipher KLEIN benchmarked on FPGA. *IEEE Transactions on Computer-Aided Design of Integrated Circuits and Systems*, 37(4):2544–2555, 2018.

[19] Rashmi Agrawal, Lake Bu, Alan Ehret, and Michel Kinsy. Open-source FPGA implementation of post-quantum cryptographic hardware primitives. In *Proceedings of 29th International Conference on Field Programmable Logic and Applications (FPL)*, Barcelona, Spain, September 2019.

[20] Rashmi Agrawal, Lake Bu, and Michel A. Kinsy. Fast arithmetic hardware library for RLWE-based homomorphic encryption. In *Proceedings of IEEE 28th Annual International Symposium on Field-Programmable Custom Computing Machines (FCCM)*, Fayetteville, AR, USA, May 2020.

[21] Masa aki Fukase, Kazunori Noda, and Tomoaki Sato. Emerging hardware cryptography and VLSI implementation. In *Proceedings of International Symposium on Intelligent Signal Processing and Communications Systems*, Bangkok, Thailand, February 2009.

[22] Raja Naeem Akram, Konstantinos Markantonakis, and Keith Mayes. User centric security model for tamper-resistant devices. In *Proceedings of IEEE 8th International Conference on e-Business Engineering*, Beijing, China, October 2011.

[23] Abdulrazzaq H. A. Al-ahdal and Nilesh K.Deshmukh. A systematic technical survey of lightweight cryptography on IoT environment. *International Journal of Scientific & Technology Research*, 9(3):6246–6261, 2020.

[24] Hussain Al-Aqrabi, Anju P. Johnson, and Richard Hill. Dynamic multiparty authentication using cryptographic hardware for the internet of things. In *Proceedings of IEEE SmartWorld, Ubiquitous Intelligence & Computing, Advanced & Trusted Computing, Scalable Computing & Communications, Cloud & Big Data Computing, Internet of People and Smart City Innovation (SmartWorld/SCALCOM/UIC/ATC/CBDCom/IOP/SCI)*, Leicester, United Kingdom, August 2019.

[25] Mohammed Al-Haidary and Qassim Nasir. Physically unclonable functions (PUFs): A systematic literature review. In *Proceedings of Advances in Science and Engineering Technology International Conferences (ASET)*, Austin, TX, USA, April 2019.

[26] Nikolaos Athanasios Anagnostopoulos, Stefan Katzenbeisser, John Chandy, and Fatemeh Tehranipoor. An overview of DRAM-based security primitives. *Cryptography*, 2(2):1–33, 2018.

[27] Kendall Ananyi, Hamad Alrimeih, and Daler Rakhmatov. Flexible hardware processor for elliptic curve cryptography over NIST prime fields. *IEEE Transactions on Very Large Scale Integration (VLSI) Systems*, 17(8):1099–1112, 2009.

[28] Ross Anderson, Mike Bond, Jolyon Clulow, and Sergei Skorobogatov. Cryptographic processors – a survey. Technical report, University of Cambridge, August 2005.

[29] Michal Andrzejczak, Farnoud Farahmand, and Kris Gaj. Full hardware implementation of the post-quantum public-key cryptography scheme round5. In *Proceedings of International Conference on ReConFigurable Computing and FPGAs (ReConFig)*, Cancun, Mexico, December 2019.

[30] F. Arnault, T. P. Berger, and A. Necer. A new class of self-synchronizing stream ciphers combining LFSR and FCSR architectures. In *Proceedings of Third International Conference on Cryptology in India (INDOCRYPT)*, Hyderabad, India, December 2002.

[31] Abu Asaduzzaman, Muhammad F. Mridh, and M. Nazim Uddin. An inexpensive plug-and-play hardware security module to restore systems from malware attacks. In *Proceedings of International Conference on Informatics, Electronics and Vision (ICIEV)*, Dhaka, Bangladesh, May 2013.

[32] M. Asghari, M. Guzman, and N. Maghari. Cross-coupled impedance based physically unclonable function (PUF) with 1.06% native instability. *IEEE Solid-State Circuits Letters*, 3(1):282–285, 2020.

[33] Armin Babaei and Gregor Schiele. Physical unclonable functions in the internet of things: State of the art and open challenges. *Sensors*, 19(14):1–18, 2019.

[34] S. Badrinarayanan, D. Khurana, R. Ostrovsky, and I. Visconti. New feasibility results in unconditional UC-secure computation with (malicious) PUFs. *IACR Cryptology ePrint Archive*, 2016.

[35] S. Badrinarayanan, D. Khurana, R. Ostrovsky, and I. Visconti. Unconditional UC-secure computation with (strongermalicious) PUFs. In *Proceedings of Annual International Conference on the Theory and Applications of Cryptographic Techniques*, April 2017.

[36] Anindita Banerjee. Reversible cryptographic hardware with optimized quantum cost and delay. In *Proceedings of Annual IEEE India Conference (INDICON)*, Kolkata, India, December 2010.

[37] Mohamed L. Barakat, Abhinav S. Mansingka, Ahmed G. Radwan, and Khaled N. Salama. Hardware stream cipher with controllable chaos generator for colour image encryption. *IET Image Processing*, 8(1):33–43, 2014.

[38] Mohamed L. Barakat, Ahmed G. Radwan, and Khaled N. Salama. Hardware realization of chaos based block cipher for image encryption. In *Proceedings of International Conference on Microelectronics (ICM)*, Hammamet, Tunisia, December 2011.

[39] D.W. Bauder. An anti-counterfeiting concept for currency systems. Technical report, Sandia National Labs, Albuquerque, NM, USA, 1983.

[40] Nathan Beckmann and Miodrag Potkonjak. Hardware-based public-key cryptography with public physically unclonable functions. In *Proceedings of International Workshop on Information Hiding*, Berlin, Heidelberg, 2009.

[41] G. Bertoni, L. Breveglieri, P. Fragneto, and G. Pelosi. Parallel hardware architectures for the cryptographic Tate pairing. In *Proceedings of Third International Conference on Information Technology: New Generations*, Las Vegas, NV, USA, April 2006.

[42] Shivam Bhasin, Jean-Luc Danger, Sylvain Guilley, Xuan Thuy Ngo, and Laurent Sauvage. Hardware trojan horses in cryptographic IP cores. In *Proceedings of*

Workshop on Fault Diagnosis and Tolerance in Cryptography, Santa Barbara, CA, USA, August 2013.

[43] Shivam Bhasin, Sylvain Guilley, and Jean-Luc Danger. From cryptography to hardware: Analyzing embedded Xilinx BRAM for cryptographic applications. In *Proceedings of 45th Annual IEEE/ACM International Symposium on Microarchitecture Workshops*, Vancouver, BC, Canada, December 2012.

[44] Rachana Bhilare, K. Harini, and Sri Adibhatla Sridevi. Ring oscillator based physically unclonable function with arbiter. In *Proceedings of International Conference on Wireless Communications, Signal Processing and Networking (WiSP-NET)*, Chennai, India, March 2018.

[45] Mohammad-Mahdi Bidmeshki, Gaurav Rajavendra Reddy, Liwei Zhou, Jeyavijayan Rajendran, and Yiorgos Makris. Hardware-based attacks to compromise the cryptographic security of an election system. In *Proceedings of IEEE 34th International Conference on Computer Design (ICCD)*, Scottsdale, AZ, USA, October 2016.

[46] Lilian Bossuet, Michael Grand, Lubos Gaspar, Viktor Fischer, and Guy Gogniat. Architectures of flexible symmetric key crypto engines—a survey: from hardware coprocessor to multi-crypto-processor system on chip. *ACM Computing Surveys*, 45(4):1–32, 2013.

[47] C. Brzuska, M. Fischlin, H. Schröder, and S. Katzenbeisser. Physically uncloneable functions in the universal composition framework. In *Proceedings of Annual Cryptology Conference*, August 2011.

[48] Christoph Böhm and Maximilian Hofer. *Physical Unclonable Functions in Theory and Practice*. Springer, 2012.

[49] Mustafa Canim, Murat Kantarcioglu, and Bradley Malin. Secure management of biomedical data with cryptographic hardware. *IEEE Transactions on Information Technology in Biomedicine*, 16(1):166–175, 2012.

[50] Yuan Cao, Le Zhang, and Chip-Hong Chang. Using image sensor PUF as root of trust for birthmarking of perceptual image hash. In *Proceedings of IEEE Asian Hardware-*

Oriented Security and Trust (AsianHOST), Yilan, Taiwan, December 2016.

[51] Hung-Ching Chang, Chun-Chin Chen, and Chih-Feng Lin. Xscale hardware acceleration on cryptographic algorithms for IPSec applications. In *Proceedings of International Conference on Information Technology: Coding and Computing*, Las Vegas, NV, USA, April 2005.

[52] Jed Kao-Tung Chang, Shaoshan Liu, Jean-Luc Gaudiot, and Chen Liu. Hardware-assisted security mechanism: The acceleration of cryptographic operations with low hardware cost. In *Proceedings of International Performance Computing and Communications Conference*, Albuquerque, NM, USA, December 2010.

[53] Urbi Chatterjee, Rajat Subhra Chakraborty, Jimson Mathew, and Dhiraj K. Pradhan. Memristor based arbiter PUF: Cryptanalysis threat and its mitigation. In *Proceedings of 29th International Conference on VLSI Design and 2016 15th International Conference on Embedded Systems (VLSID)*, Kolkata, India, January 2016.

[54] Anupam Chattopadhyay, Ayesha Khalid, Subhamoy Maitra, and Shashwat Raizada. Designing high-throughput hardware accelerator for stream cipher HC-128. In *Proceedings of IEEE International Symposium on Circuits and Systems (ISCAS)*, Seoul, South Korea, May 2012.

[55] Anupam Chattopadhyay and Goutam Paul. Exploring security-performance trade-offs during hardware accelerator design of stream cipher RC4. In *Proceedings of IEEE/IFIP 20th International Conference on VLSI and System-on-Chip (VLSI-SoC)*, Santa Cruz, CA, USA, October 2012.

[56] Wenjie Che, Fareena Saqib, and Jim Plusquellic. Novel offset techniques for improving bitstring quality of a hardware-embedded delay PUF. *IEEE Transactions on Very Large Scale Integration (VLSI) Systems*, 26(4):733–743, 2018.

[57] Chien-Ming Chen, Tsu-Yang Wu, Bing-Zhe He, and Hung-Min Sun. An efficient time-bound hierarchical key management scheme without tamper-resistant devices. In *Proceedings of International Conference on Computing, Measure-*

ment, Control and Sensor Network, Taiyuan, China, July 2012.

[58] Xiaoming Chen, Boxun Li, Yu Wang, Yongpan Liu, and Huazhong Yang. A unified methodology for designing hardware random number generators based on any probability distribution. *IEEE Transactions on Circuits and Systems II: Express Briefs*, 63(8):783–787, 2016.

[59] Huiju Cheng and Howard M. Heys. Compact hardware implementation of the block cipher camellia with concurrent error detection. In *Proceedings of Canadian Conference on Electrical and Computer Engineering*, Vancouver, BC, Canada, April 2007.

[60] Ray C. C. Cheung, Dong-U Lee, Wayne Luk, and John D. Villasenor. Hardware generation of arbitrary random number distributions from uniform distributions via the inversion method. *IEEE Transactions on Very Large Scale Integration (VLSI) Systems*, 15(8):952–962, 2007.

[61] Kang-Un Choi, Seungbum Baek, Jino Heo, and Jong-Phil Hong. A 100% stable sense-amplifier-based physically unclonable function with individually embedded non-volatile memory. *IEEE Access*, 8:21857–21865, 2020.

[62] Piljoo Choi, Jeong-Taek Kong, and Dong Kyue Kim. Analysis of hardware modular inversion modules for elliptic curve cryptography. In *Proceedings of International SoC Design Conference (ISOCC)*, Gyungju, South Korea, November 2015.

[63] Xin Chuan, Yingjian Yan, and Yilun Zhang. An efficient triggering method of hardware trojan in AES cryptographic circuit. In *Proceedings of 2nd IEEE International Conference on Integrated Circuits and Microsystems (ICICM)*, Nanjing, China, November 2017.

[64] K.-H. Chuang, E. Bury, R. Degraeve, B. Kaczer, G. Groeseneken, I. Verbauwhede, and D. Linten. Physically unclonable function using CMOS breakdown position. In *Proceedings of IEEE International Reliability Physics Symposium (IRPS)*, Monterey, CA, USA, April 2017.

[65] Alessandro Cilardo and Nicola Mazzocca. Exploiting vulnerabilities in cryptographic hash functions based on reconfigurable hardware. *IEEE Transactions on Information Forensics and Security*, 8(5):810–820, 2013.

[66] Alessandro Cilardo and Nicola Mazzocca. Exploiting vulnerabilities in cryptographic hash functions based on reconfigurable hardware. *IEEE Transactions on Information Forensics and Security*, 8(5):810–820, 2013.

[67] Peter Clarke. London calling: Security technology takes time. *EE Times (UBM Tech Electronics)*, 2013.

[68] Bernard Colbert, Anthony H. Dekker, and Lynn Margaret Batten. Heraclitus: A LFSR-based stream cipher with key dependent structure. In *Proceedings of International Conference on Communications and Signal Processing*, Calicut, India, February 2011.

[69] Brice Colombier, Lilian Bossuet, Viktor Fischer, and David Hély. Key reconciliation protocols for error correction of silicon PUF responses. *IEEE Transactions on Information Forensics and Security*, 12(8):1988–2002, 2017.

[70] F. Crowe, A. Daly, T. Kerins, and W. Marnane. Single-chip FPGA implementation of a cryptographic co-processor. In *Proceedings of IEEE International Conference on Field- Programmable Technology*, Brisbane, NSW, Australia, December 2004.

[71] Tyler Cultice, Carson Labrado, and Himanshu Thapliyal. A PUF based CAN security framework. In *Proceedings of IEEE Computer Society Annual Symposium on VLSI (ISVLSI)*, Limassol, Cyprus, July 2020.

[72] D. Dachman-Soled, N. Fleischhacker, J. Katz, A. Lysyanskaya, and D. Schröder. Feasibility and infeasibility of secure computation with malicious PUFs. In *Proceedings of Annual Cryptology Conference*, August 2014.

[73] I. Damaj, M. Itani, and H. Diab. Serpent cryptography on static and dynamic reconfigurable hardware. In *Proceedings of IEEE International Conference on Computer Systems and Applications*, Dubai, UAE, March 2006.

[74] I. Damgård and A. Scafuro. Unconditionally secure and universally composable commitments from physical assumptions. In *Proceedings of International Conference on the Theory and Application of Cryptology and Information Security*, December 2013.

[75] Viet B. Dang, Farnoud Farahmand, Michal Andrzejczak, and Kris Gaj. Implementing and benchmarking three lattice-based post-quantum cryptography algorithms using software/hardware codesign. In *Proceedings of International Conference on Field-Programmable Technology (ICFPT)*, Tianjin, China, December 2019.

[76] Jayita Das, Kevin Scott, Drew Burgett, Srinath Rajaram, and Sanjukta Bhanja. A novel geometry based MRAM PUF. In *Proceedings of IEEE International Conference on Nanotechnology*, Toronto, Ontario, Canada, August 2014.

[77] Guerric Meurice de Dormale and Jean-Jacques Quisquater. High-speed hardware implementations of elliptic curve cryptography: A survey. *Journal of Systems Architecture*, 53(3):72–84, 2007.

[78] L. de Macedo Mourelle and N. Nedjah. Efficient cryptographic hardware using the co-design methodology. In *Proceedings of International Conference on Information Technology: Coding and Computing*, Las Vegas, NV, USA, April 2004.

[79] Otávio de Souza Martins Gomes and Robson Luiz Moreno. A compact 128-bits symmetric cryptography hardware module. In *Proceedings of 8th International Conference on Information Technology and Electrical Engineering (ICITEE)*, Yogyakarta, Indonesia, October 2016.

[80] Otávio de Souza Martins Gomes and Robson Luiz Moreno. A compact S-box module for 128/192/256-bit symmetric cryptography hardware. In *Proceedings of 9th International Conference on Developments in eSystems Engineering (DeSE)*, Liverpool, UK, August 2016.

[81] Jeroen Delvaux, Dawu Gu, Dries Schellekens, and Ingrid Verbauwhede. Helper data algorithms for PUF-based key generation: Overview and analysis. *IEEE Transactions on*

Computer-Aided Design of Integrated Circuits and Systems, 34(6):889–902, 2015.

[82] Jeroen Delvaux, Roel Peeters, Dawu Gu, and Ingrid Verbauwhede. A survey on lightweight entity authentication with strong PUFs. *ACM Computing Surveys (CSUR)*, 48(2):26:1–26:42, 2015.

[83] Soumyabrata Dev and Ziaul Haque Choudhury. A randomized cryptographic algorithm and its simulation in C and MATLAB with its hardware implementation in Verilog HDL. In *Proceedings of 3rd International Conference on Anti-counterfeiting, Security, and Identification in Communication*, Hong Kong, China, August 2009.

[84] Imed Ben Dhaou, Tuan Nguyen Gia, Pasi Liljeberg, and Hannu Tenhunen. Low-latency hardware architecture for cipher-based message authentication code. In *Proceedings of IEEE International Symposium on Circuits and Systems (ISCAS)*, Baltimore, MD, USA, May 2017.

[85] C. Dhoha, S. Ben Othman, and S. Ben Saoud. An FPGA hardware implementation of the Rijndael block cipher. In *Proceedings of International Conference on Design and Test of Integrated Systems in Nanoscale Technology*, Tunis, Tunisia, September 2006.

[86] William Diehl, Farnoud Farahmand, Panasayya Yalla, Jens-Peter Kaps, and Kris Gaj. Comparison of hardware and software implementations of selected lightweight block ciphers. In *Proceedings of 27th International Conference on Field Programmable Logic and Applications (FPL)*, Ghent, Belgium, September 2017.

[87] Yarkın Doroz, Erdinç Ozturk, and Berk Sunar. Accelerating fully homomorphic encryption in hardware. *IEEE Transactions on Computers*, 64(6):1509–1521, 2015.

[88] Cheng-Hua Duan, Jun Jiang, Xing-Ming Wang, and Wen-Yuan Xu. Fast S-box substitution instructions and their hardware implementation for accelerating symmetric cryptographic processing. In *Proceedings of International Conference on E-Business and Information System Security*, Wuhan, China, May 2009.

[89] Kavyashree Puttananj egowda and Sylvia Thomas. A detailed review on physical unclonable function circuits for hardware security. In *Proceedings of IEEE 9th Annual Information Technology, Electronics and Mobile Communication Conference (IEMCON)*, Vancouver, BC, Canada, November 2018.

[90] Susana Eiroa, Iluminada Baturone, Antonio J. Acosta, and Jorge Dávila. Using physical unclonable functions for hardware authentication: A survey. In *Proceedings of XXV Conference on Design of Circuits and Integrated Systems*, Lazarote, Spain, November 2010.

[91] Thomas Eisenbarth, Christof Paar, Axel Poschmann, Sandeep Kumar, and Leif Uhsadel. A survey of lightweight-cryptography implementations. *IEEE Design and Test of Computers*, 24(6):522–533, 2007.

[92] R. Elbaz, L. Torres, G. Sassatelli, P. Guillemin, C. Anguille C. Buatois, and J. B. Rigaud. Hardware engines for bus encryption: a survey of existing techniques. In *Proceedings of the Design, Automation and Test in Europe Conference and Exhibition*, San Diego, CA, USA, June 2005.

[93] Beomsoo Park, Mark Tehranipoor, Domenic Forte, and Nima Maghari. A metal-via resistance based physically unclonable function with 1.18% native instability. In *Proceedings of IEEE Custom Integrated Circuits Conference (CICC)*, Austin, TX, USA, April 2019.

[94] Abbas Fairouz, Monther Abusultan, Viacheslav Fedorov, and Sunil Khatri. Hardware acceleration of hash operations in modern microprocessors. *IEEE Transactions on Computers (Early Access Article)*, pages 1–1, 2020.

[95] Farnoud Farahmand, Duc Tri Nguyen, Viet B. Dang, Ahmed Ferozpuri, and Kris Gaj. Software/hardware codesign of the post quantum cryptography algorithm NTRUEncrypt using high-level synthesis and register-transfer level design methodologies. In *Proceedings of International Conference on Field Programmable Logic and Applications (FPL)*, Barcelona, Spain, September 2019.

[96] Lifeng Feng, Xiaofeng Wang, and Yingjue Fang. An improved algorithm of stream cipher based on LFSR. In *Proceedings of 8th International Conference on Wireless Communications, Networking and Mobile Computing*, Shanghai, China, September 2012.

[97] Alberto Ferrante. *A Design Methodology for HW/SW Security Protocols*. PhD thesis, Department of Information Technology, University of Milan, March 2006.

[98] S. Fields and D. Bouldin. Cryptographic key protection module in hardware for the need2know system. In *Proceedings of 48th Midwest Symposium on Circuits and Systems*, Covington, KY, USA, August 2005.

[99] Russell A. Fink, Alan T. Sherman, and Richard Carback. Tpm meets DRE: Reducing the trust base for electronic voting using trusted platform modules. *IEEE Transactions on Information Forensics and Security*, 4(4):628–637, 2009.

[100] Russell A. Fink, Alan T. Sherman, and Richard Carback. Corrections to "TPM meets DRE: Reducing the trust base for electronic voting using trusted platform modules" [dec 09 628-637]. *IEEE Transactions on Information Forensics and Security*, 5(1):194–194, 2010.

[101] Bruno Forlin, Ronaldo Husemann, Luigi Carro, Cezar Reinbrecht, Said Hamdioui, and Mottaqiallah Taouil. G-PUF: An intrinsic PUF based on gpu error signatures. In *Proceedings of IEEE European Test Symposium (ETS)*, Tallinn, Estonia, May 2020.

[102] J.J.A. Fournier and S. Moore. Hardware-software codesign of a vector co-processor for public key cryptography. In *Proceedings of 9th EUROMICRO Conference on Digital System Design*, Dubrovnik, Croatia, August 2006.

[103] Daniele Fronte, Annie Perez, and Eric Payrat. Celator: A multi-algorithm cryptographic co-processor. In *Proceedings of International Conference on Reconfigurable Computing and FPGAs*, Cancun, Mexico, December 2008.

[104] M. Fukase, R. Akaoka, Liu Lei, Cheng Tong Shu, and T. Sato. Hardware cryptography for ubiquitous computing.

In *Proceedings of IEEE International Symposium on Communications and Information Technology*, Beijing, China, October 2005.

[105] Kris Gaj, Jens-Peter Kaps, Venkata Amirineni, Marcin Rogawski, Ekawat Homsirikamol, and Benjamin Y. Brewster. Athena - automated tool for hardware evaluation: Toward fair and comprehensive benchmarking of cryptographic hardware using FPGAs. In *Proceedings of International Conference on Field Programmable Logic and Applications*, Milano, Italy, August 2010.

[106] M.D. Galanis, P. Kitsos, G. Kostopoulos, N. Sklavos, O. Koufopavlou, and C.E. Goutis. Comparison of the hardware architectures and FPGA implementations of stream ciphers. In *Proceedings of the 2004 11th IEEE International Conference on Electronics, Circuits and Systems*, Tel Aviv, Israel, December 2004.

[107] T.S. Ganesh and T.S.B. Sudarshan. ASIC implementation of a unified hardware architecture for non-key based cryptographic hash primitives. In *Proceedings of International Conference on Information Technology: Coding and Computing*, Las Vegas, NV, USA, April 2005.

[108] T.S. Ganesh, T.S.B. Sudarshan, N.K. Srinivasan, and K. Jayapal. Pre-silicon prototyping of a unified hardware architecture for cryptographic manipulation detection codes. In *Proceedings of IEEE International Conference on Field-Programmable Technology*, Brisbane, NSW, Australia, December 2004.

[109] Fatemeh Ganji. *On the Learnability of Physically Unclonable Functions (T-Labs Series in Telecommunication Services)*. Springer, 2018.

[110] Yansong Gao, Damith C. Ranasinghe, Said F. Al-Sarawi, Omid Kavehei, and Derek Abbott. Emerging physical unclonable functions with nanotechnology. *IEEE Access*, 4:61–80, 2016.

[111] M. Garcia-Bosque, C. Sánchez-Azqueta, G. Royo, and S. Celma. Lightweight ciphers based on chaotic map - lfsr architectures. In *Proceedings of 12th Conference on Ph.D.*

Research in Microelectronics and Electronics (PRIME), Lisbon, Portugal, June 2016.

[112] Achiranshu Garg and Tony T. Kim. Design of SRAM PUF with improved uniformity and reliability utilizing device aging effect. In *Proceedings of IEEE International Symposium on Circuits and Systems (ISCAS)*, Melbourne VIC, Australia, June 2014.

[113] Blaise Gassend, Dwaine Clarke, Marten van Dijk and Srinivas Devadas. Silicon physical random functions. In *Proceedings of the Computer and Communications Security Conference*, November 2002.

[114] Michael Gautschi, Michael Muehlberghuber, Andreas Traber, Sven Stucki, Matthias Baer, Renzo Andri, Luca Benini, Beat Muheim, and Hubert Kaeslin. SIR10US: A tightly coupled elliptic-curve cryptography co-processor for the Open-RISC. In *Proceedings of IEEE 25th International Conference on Application-Specific Systems, Architectures and Processors*, Zurich, Switzerland, June 2014.

[115] Santosh Ghosh. Design and analysis of pairing based cryptographic hardware for prime fields. In *Proceedings of IEEE Computer Society Annual Symposium on VLSI*, Chennai, India, July 2011.

[116] Weihan Goh, Peng Chor Leong, and Chai Kiat Yeo. A plausibly-deniable, practical trusted platform module based anti-forensics client-server system. *IEEE Journal on Selected Areas in Communications*, 29(7):1377–1391, 2011.

[117] Otávio S. M. Gomes, Robson L. Moreno, and Tales C. Pimenta. A fast cryptography pipelined hardware developed in FPGA with VHDL. In *Proceedings of 3rd International Congress on Ultra Modern Telecommunications and Control Systems and Workshops (ICUMT)*, Budapest, Hungary, October 2011.

[118] R. Granger, D. Page, and M. Stam. Hardware and software normal basis arithmetic for pairing-based cryptography in characteristic three. *IEEE Transactions on Computers*, 54(7):852–860, 2005.

[119] Ricardo Graves, Giorgio Di Natale, Lejla Batina, Shivam Bhasin, Baris Ege, Apostolos Fournaris, Nele Mentens, Stjepan Picek, Francesco Regazzoni, Vladimir Rozic, Nicolas Sklavos, and Bohan Yang. Challenges in designing trustworthy cryptographic co-processors. In *Proceedings of IEEE International Symposium on Circuits and Systems (ISCAS)*, Lisbon, Portugal, May 2015.

[120] Chongyan Gu, Weiqiang Liu, Neil Hanley, Robert Hesselbarth, and Máire O'Neill. A theoretical model to link uniqueness and min-entropy for PUF evaluations. *IEEE Transactions on Computers*, 68(2):287–293, 2019.

[121] J. Guajardo, S. S. Kumar, G. J. Schrijen, and P. Tuyls. FPGA intrinsic PUFs and their use for IP protection. In *Proceedings of*, September. Paillier P., Verbauwhede I. (eds) Cryptographic Hardware and Embedded Systems - CHES 2007. CHES 2007. Lecture Notes in Computer Science, vol 4727. Springer, Berlin, Heidelberg.

[122] Sylvain Guilley, Laurent Sauvage, Jean-Luc Danger, and Philippe Hoogvorst. Area optimization of cryptographic co-processors implemented in dual-rail with precharge positive logic. In *Proceedings of International Conference on Field Programmable Logic and Applications*, Heidelberg, Germany, September 2008.

[123] Sourav Sen Gupta, Anupam Chattopadhyay, Koushik Sinha, Subhamoy Maitra, and Bhabani P. Sinha. High-performance hardware implementation for RC4 stream cipher. *IEEE Transactions on Computers*, 62(4):730–743, 2013.

[124] Basel Halak. *Physically Unclonable Functions: From Basic Design Principles to Advanced Hardware Security Applications*. Springer International Publishing, 2018.

[125] Basel Halak, Said Subhan Waizi, and Asad Islam. A survey of hardware implementations of elliptic curve cryptographic systems. *Cryptology ePrint Archive*, 2016.

[126] Helena Handschuh. Hardware intrinsic security based on SRAM PUFs: Tales from the industry. In *Proceedings of IEEE International Symposium on Hardware-Oriented Security and Trust*, San Diego CA, USA, June 2011.

[127] Neil Hanley and Maire ONeill. Hardware comparison of the ISO/IEC 29192-2 block ciphers. In *Proceedings of IEEE Computer Society Annual Symposium on VLSI*, Amherst, MA, USA, August 2012.

[128] L. Henzen, F. Carbognani, N. Felber, and W. Fichtner. VLSI hardware evaluation of the stream ciphers Salsa20 and ChaCha, and the compression function Rumba. In *Proceedings of 2nd International Conference on Signals, Circuits and Systems*, Monastir, Tunisia, November 2008.

[129] L. Henzen, F. Carbognani, N. Felber, and W. Fichtner. Hardware evaluation of the stream cipher-based hash functions RadioGatún and irRUPT. In *Proceedings of Design, Automation & Test in Europe Conference & Exhibition*, Nice, France, April 2009.

[130] Charles Herder, Meng-Day Yu, Farinaz Koushanfar, and Srinivas Devadas. Physical unclonable functions and applications: A tutorial. *Proceedings of the IEEE*, 102(8):1126 – 1141, 2014.

[131] Andreas Herkle, Joachim Becker, and Maurits Ortmanns. An arbiter PUF employing eye-opening oscillation for improved noise suppression. In *Proceedings of IEEE International Symposium on Circuits and Systems (ISCAS)*, Florence, Italy, May 2018.

[132] Sebastian Hessel, David Szczesny, Nils Lohmann, Attila Bilgic, and Josef Hausner. Implementation and benchmarking of hardware accelerators for ciphering in LTE terminals. In *Proceedings of GLOBECOM 2009 - 2009 IEEE Global Telecommunications Conference*, Honolulu, HI, USA, December 2009.

[133] Matthias Hiller, Dominik Merli, Frederic Stumpf, and Georg Sigl. Complementary IBS: Application specific error correction for PUFs. In *Proceedings of IEEE International Symposium on Hardware-Oriented Security and Trust*, San Francisco, CA, USA, June 2012.

[134] Toru Hisakado, Nobuyuki Kobayashi, Satoshi Goto, Kunihiko Higashi, Ichiro Kitao, and Yukiyasu Tsunoo. 61.5mw 2048-bit RSA cryptographic co-processor lsi based on n bitwised modular multiplier. In *Proceedings of International*

Symposium on VLSI Design, Automation and Test, Hsinchu, Taiwan, April 2006.

[135] Andrea Hoeller and Ronald Toegl. Trusted platform modules in cyber-physical systems: On the interference between security and dependability. In *Proceedings of IEEE European Symposium on Security and Privacy Workshops (EuroS&PW)*, London, UK, April 2018.

[136] Naofumi Homma, Kazuya Saito, and Takafumi Aoki. Toward formal design of practical cryptographic hardware based on Galois field arithmetic. *IEEE Transactions on Computers*, 63(10):2604–2613, 2014.

[137] Jaber Hosseinzadeh and Maghsoud hosseinzadeh. A comprehensive survey on evaluation of lightweight symmetric ciphers: Hardware and software implementation. *Advances in Computer Science: An International Journal*, 5(5):31–41, 2016.

[138] Hilal Houssain, Mohamad Badra, and Turki F. Al-Somani. Hardware implementations of elliptic curve cryptography in wireless sensor networks. In *Proceedings of International Conference for Internet Technology and Secured Transactions*, Abu Dhabi, United Arab Emirates, December 2011.

[139] A.L. Huang and W.T. Penzhorn. Cryptographic hash functions and low-power techniques for embedded hardware. In *Proceedings of the IEEE International Symposium on Industrial Electronics*, Dubrovnik, Croatia, June 2005.

[140] Miaoqing Huang and Shiming Li. A delay-based PUF design using multiplexers on FPGA. In *Proceedings of IEEE 21st Annual International Symposium on Field-Programmable Custom Computing Machines*, Seattle, WA, USA, April 2013.

[141] Michal Hulic, Liberios Vokorokos, Norbert Ádám, and Peter Fecil'ak. Hardware design of cryptographic accelerator. In *Proceedings of IEEE 16th World Symposium on Applied Machine Intelligence and Informatics (SAMI)*, Kosice, Slovakia, February 2018.

[142] William Hupp, Adarsh Hasandka, Ricardo Siqueira de Carvalho, and Danish Saleem. Module-OT: A hardware security module for operational technology. In *Proceedings of IEEE*

Texas Power and Energy Conference (TPEC), College Station, TX, USA, February 2020.

[143] Tanya Ignatenko and Frans Willems. Achieving secure fuzzy commitment scheme for optical PUFs. In *Proceedings of Fifth International Conference on Intelligent Information Hiding and Multimedia Signal Processing*, Kyoto, Japan, September 2009.

[144] Malik Imran, Muhammad Kashif, and Muhammad Rashid. Hardware design and implementation of scalar multiplication in elliptic curve cryptography (ECC) over gf(2^{163}) on FPGA. In *Proceedings of International Conference on Information and Communication Technologies (ICICT)*, Karachi, Pakistan, December 2015.

[145] MD. Mainul Islam, MD. Selim Hossain, MD. Shahjalal, MOH. Khalid Hasan, and Yeong Min Jang. Area-time efficient hardware implementation of modular multiplication for elliptic curve cryptography. *IEEE Access*, 8:73898–73906, 2020.

[146] C. Jaeger, M. Algasinger, U. Rührmair, G. Csaba, and M. Stutzmann. Random pn-junctions for physical cryptography. *Applied Physics Letters*, 96(17), 2010.

[147] Mohita Jaiswal and Kusum Lata. Hardware implementation of text encryption using elliptic curve cryptography over 192 bit prime field. In *Proceedings of International Conference on Advances in Computing, Communications and Informatics (ICACCI)*, Bangalore, India, September 2018.

[148] T. Jamil and A. Ahmad. An investigation into the application of linear feedback shift registers for steganography. In *Proceedings of IEEE Southeast Conference*, Columbia, SC, USA, August 2002.

[149] Biswapati Jana, Shyamal Kumar Mondal, Shannistha Jana, and Debasis Giri. Cheating prevention in visual cryptographic schemes using message embedding: A hardware based practical approach. In *Proceedings of International Conference on Issues and Challenges in Intelligent Computing Techniques (ICICT)*, Ghaziabad, India, February 2014.

[150] K. Naveen Jarold, P. Karthigaikumar, N.M. Sivamangai, R. Sandhya, and Sruthi B. Asok. Hardware implementation of dna based cryptography. In *Proceedings of 2013 IEEE Conference on Information & Communication Technologies*, Thuckalay, Tamil Nadu, India, April 2013.

[151] Dan Jiang and Cheun Ngen Chong. Anti-counterfeiting using phosphor PUF. In *Proceedings of 2nd International Conference on Anti-counterfeiting, Security and Identification*, Guiyang, China, August 2008.

[152] N. Joshi, Kaijie Wu, J. Sundararajan, and R. Karri. Concurrent error detection for involutional functions with applications in fault-tolerant cryptographic hardware design. *IEEE Transactions on Computer-Aided Design of Integrated Circuits and Systems*, 25(6):1163–1169, 2006.

[153] K. K. Lofstrom, W.R. Daasch, and D. Taylor. IC identification circuit using device mismatch. In *Proceedings of IEEE International Solid-State Circuits Conference*, February 2000.

[154] S.C. Kak. Secret-hardware public-key cryptography. *EE Proceedings E-Computers and Digital Techniques*, 133(2):94–96, 1986.

[155] A.P. Kakarountas, H. Michail, C.E. Goutis, and C. Efstathiou. Implementation of HSSec: a high–speed cryptographic co-processor. In *Proceedings of IEEE Conference on Emerging Technologies and Factory Automation*, Patras, Greece, September 2007.

[156] Christiana Kapatsori, Yu Liu, Angelos Antonopoulos, and Yiorgos Makris. Hardware dithering: A run-time method for trojan neutralization in wireless cryptographic ICs. In *Proceedings of*, Phoenix, AZ, USA, October 2018.

[157] Muhammad Kashif, Ihsan Cicek, and Malik Imran. A hardware efficient elliptic curve accelerator for FPGA based cryptographic applications. In *Proceedings of 11th International Conference on Electrical and Electronics Engineering (ELECO)*, Bursa, Turkey, November 2019.

[158] Amandeep Kaur, Harsh Kumar Verma, and Ravindra Kumar Singh. 3d — playfair cipher using LFSR based unique random number generator. In *Proceedings of Sixth International*

Conference on Contemporary Computing (IC3), Noida, India, August 2013.

[159] Masoud Kaveh and Mohamad Reza Mosavi. A lightweight mutual authentication for smart grid neighborhood area network communications based on physically unclonable function. *IEEE Systems Journal (Early Access Article)*, pages 1–10, 2020.

[160] Mehran Mozaffari Kermani and Reza Azarderakhsh. Lightweight hardware architectures for fault diagnosis schemes of efficiently-maskable cryptographic substitution boxes. In *Proceedings of IEEE International Conference on Electronics, Circuits and Systems (ICECS)*, Monte Carlo, Monaco, December 2016.

[161] Ayesha Khalid, Goutam Paul, and Anupam Chattopadhyay. RC4-AccSuite: A hardware acceleration suite for RC4-like stream ciphers. *IEEE Transactions on Very Large Scale Integration (VLSI) Systems*, 25(3):1072–1084, 2017.

[162] Mohamed Khalil-Hani, Arif Irwansyah, and Y.W. Hau. A tightly coupled finite field arithmetic hardware in an FPGA-based embedded processor core for elliptic curve cryptography. In *Proceedings of International Conference on Electronic Design*, Penang, Malaysia, December 2008.

[163] Mohamed Khalil-Hani, Vishnu P. Nambiar, and M. N. Marsono. Hardware acceleration of OpenSSL cryptographic functions for high-performance internet security. In *Proceedings of International Conference on Intelligent Systems, Modelling and Simulation*, Liverpool, UK, January 2010.

[164] Daewon Kim, Yongsung Jeon, and Jeongnyeo Kim. A secure channel establishment method on a hardware security module. In *Proceedings of International Conference on Information and Communication Technology Convergence (ICTC)*, Busan, South Korea, October 2014.

[165] Jeong-Hyeon Kim, Ho-Jun Jo, Kyung-Kuk Jo, Sung-Hee Cho, Jae-Yong Chung, and Joon-Sung Yang. Reliable and lightweight PUF-based key generation using various index voting architecture. In *Proceedings of Design, Automation & Test in Europe Conference & Exhibition (DATE)*, Grenoble, France, March 2020.

[166] Sunwoong Kim, Keewoo Lee, Wonhee Cho, Yujin Nam, Jung Hee Cheon, and Rob A. Rutenbar. Hardware architecture of a number theoretic transform for a bootstrappable RNS-based homomorphic encryption scheme. In *Proceedings of IEEE 28th Annual International Symposium on Field-Programmable Custom Computing Machines (FCCM)*, Fayetteville, AR, USA, May 2020.

[167] P. Kitsos, M.D. Galanis, and O. Koufopavlou. High-speed hardware implementations of the KASUMI block cipher. In *Proceedings of IEEE International Symposium on Circuits and Systems*, Vancouver, BC, Canada, May 2004.

[168] P. Kitsos, G. Kostopoulos, N. Sklavos, and O. Koufopavlou. Hardware implementation of the RC4 stream cipher. In *Proceedings of 46th Midwest Symposium on Circuits and Systems*, Cairo, Egypt, December 2003.

[169] P. Kitsos and O. Koufopavlou. A time and area efficient hardware implementation of the MISTY1 block cipher. In *Proceedings of 46th Midwest Symposium on Circuits and Systems*, Cairo, Egypt, December 2003.

[170] P. Kitsos and O. Koufopavlou. Efficient architecture and hardware implementation of the whirlpool hash function. *IEEE Transactions on Consumer Electronics*, 50(1):208–213, 2004.

[171] Paris Kitsos and Ulrich Kaiser. A high-speed hardware implementation of the Hermes8-128 stream cipher. In *Proceedings of 18th European Conference on Circuit Theory and Design*, Seville, Spain, August 2007.

[172] Paris Kitsos, George Selimis, Odysseas Koufopavlou, and Athanassios N. Skodras. A hardware implementation of Curupira block cipher for wireless sensors. In *Proceedings of 11th EUROMICRO Conference on Digital System Design Architectures, Methods and Tools*, Parma, Italy, September 2008.

[173] Alexander Klimm, Oliver Sander, and Jurgen Becker. A microblaze specific co-processor for real-time hyperelliptic curve cryptography on Xilinx FPGA. In *Proceedings of IEEE International Symposium on Parallel & Distributed Processing*, Rome, Italy, May 2009.

[174] R. Kousalya and G.A. Sathish Kumar. A survey of lightweight cryptographic algorithm for information security and hardware efficiency in resource constrained devices. In *Proceedings of International Conference on Vision Towards Emerging Trends in Communication and Networking (ViTE-CoN)*, Vellore, India, March 2019.

[175] Anoop Koyily. A study on modeling of MUX-based physical unclonable functions. Master's thesis, University of Minnesota Twin Cities, Twin Cities, Minnesota, USA, 2018.

[176] Brian Koziel, A-Bon Ackie, Rami El Khatib, Reza Azarderakhsh, and Mehran Mozaffari Kermani. Sike'd up: Fast hardware architectures for supersingular isogeny key encapsulation. *IEEE Transactions on Circuits and Systems I: Regular Papers (Early Access Article)*, pages 1–13, 2020.

[177] Brian Koziel, Reza Azarderakhsh, and Mehran Mozaffari Kermani. A high-performance and scalable hardware architecture for isogeny-based cryptography. *IEEE Transactions on Computers*, 67(11):1594–1609, 2018.

[178] Hugo Krawczyk. LFSR-based hashing and authentication. In *Proceedings of*, Desmedt Y.G. (eds) Advances in Cryptology – CRYPTO '94. CRYPTO 1994. Lecture Notes in Computer Science, vol 839. Springer, Berlin, Heidelberg.

[179] Takeshi Kumaki, Masaya Yoshikawa, and Takeshi Fujino. Cipher-destroying and secret-key-emitting hardware trojan against AES core. In *Proceedings of IEEE 56th International Midwest Symposium on Circuits and Systems (MWSCAS)*, Columbus, OH, USA, August 2013.

[180] Keshav Kumar, K.R. Ramkumar, Amanpreet Kaur, and Somanshu Choudhary. A survey on hardware implementation of cryptographic algorithms using field programmable gate array. In *Proceedings of IEEE 9th International Conference on Communication Systems and Network Technologies (CSNT)*, Gwalior, India, April 2020.

[181] Nitish Kumar, Jialuo Chen, Monodeep Kar, Suresh K. Sitaraman, Saibal Mukhopadhyay, and Satish Kumar. Multigated carbon nanotube field effect transistors-based physically unclonable functions as security keys. *IEEE Internet of Things Journal*, 6(1):325–334, 2019.

[182] Raghavan Kumar, Philipp Jovanovic, Wayne Burleson, and Ilia Polian. Parametric trojans for fault-injection attacks on cryptographic hardware. In *Proceedings of Workshop on Fault Diagnosis and Tolerance in Cryptography*, Busan, South Korea, September 2014.

[183] S. Dinesh Kumar, Carson Labrado, Riasad Badhan, Himanshu Thapliyal, and Vijay Singh. Solar cell based physically unclonable function for cybersecurity in IoT devices. In *Proceedings of IEEE Computer Society Annual Symposium on VLSI (ISVLSI)*, Hong Kong, China, July 2018.

[184] Anil Kumar Kurra and Usha Rani Nelakuditi. A secure arbiter physical unclonable functions (PUFs) for device authentication and identification. *Indonesian Journal of Electrical Engineering and Informatics (IJEEI)*, 7(1), 2019.

[185] K.G.P. Kurup, M. Devarajan, and S. Sathyanarayana. Static charge measurements on PUF/PIR materials. In *Proceedings of International Conference on Electromagnetic Interference and Compatibility*, Chennai, India, December 2003.

[186] Giray Kömürcü, Ali Emre Pusane, and Günhan Dünda. Analysis of ring oscillator structures to develop a design methodology for RO-PUF circuits. In *Proceedings of IFIP/IEEE 21st International Conference on Very Large Scale Integration (VLSI-SoC)*, Istanbul, Turkey, October 2013.

[187] Benedikt Köppel and Stephan Neuhaus. Analysis of a hardware security module's high-availability setting. *IEEE Security & Privacy*, 11(3):77–80, 2013.

[188] Carlos Andres Lara-Nino, Arturo Diaz-Perez, and Miguel Morales-Sandoval. Lightweight hardware architectures for the present cipher in FPGA. *IEEE Transactions on Circuits and Systems I: Regular Papers*, 64(9):1072–1084, 2017.

[189] Carlos Andres Lara-Nino, Miguel Morales-Sandoval, and Arturo Diaz-Perez. Novel FPGA-based low-cost hardware architecture for the present block cipher. In *Proceedings of Euromicro Conference on Digital System Design (DSD)*, Limassol, Cyprus, September 2016.

[190] Ana Lasheras, Ramon Canal, Eva Rodríguez, and Luca Cassano. Lightweight protection of cryptographic hardware accelerators against differential fault analysis. In *Proceedings of IEEE 26th International Symposium on On-Line Testing and Robust System Design (IOLTS)*, Napoli, Italy, July 2020.

[191] Ralf Laue, H. Gregor Molter, Felix Rieder, Sorin A. Huss, and Kartik Saxena. A novel multiple core co-processor architecture for efficient server-based public key cryptographic applications. In *Proceedings of IEEE Computer Society Annual Symposium on VLSI*, Montpellier, France, April 2008.

[192] J. W. Lee, D. Lim, B. Gassend, G. E. Suh, M. Van Dijk, and S. Devadas. A technique to build a secret key in integrated circuits for identification and authentication applications. In *Proceedings of Symposium on VLSI Circuits. Digest of Technical Papers*, June 2004.

[193] Jongmin Lee, Minsun Kim, Gicheol Shin, and Yoonmyung Lee. A 20f2 area-efficient differential NAND-structured physically unclonable function for low-cost IoT security. *IEEE Solid-State Circuits Letters*, 2(9):139–142, 2019.

[194] Jongmin Lee, Donghyeon Lee, Yongmin Lee, and Yoonmyung Lee. A 445f2 leakage-based physically unclonable function with lossless stabilization through remapping for IoT security. In *Proceedings of IEEE International Solid - State Circuits Conference - (ISSCC)*, San Francisco, CA, USA, February 2018.

[195] Sang Muk Lee, Eun Nu Ri Ko, and Seung Eun Lee. A hardware scheduler for multicore block cipher processor. In *Proceedings of 24th Euromicro International Conference on Parallel, Distributed, and Network-Based Processing (PDP)*, Heraklion, Greece, February 2016.

[196] Congwu Li, Le Guan, Jingqiang Lin, Bo Luo, Quanwei Cai, Jiwu Jing, and Jing Wang. Mimosa: Protecting private keys against memory disclosure attacks using hardware transactional memory. *IEEE Transactions on Dependable and Secure Computing (Early Access Article)*, pages 1–1, 2019.

[197] Dai Li and Kaiyuan Yang. A self-regulated and reconfigurable CMOS physically unclonable function featuring zero-

overhead stabilization. *IEEE Journal of Solid-State Circuits*, 55(1):98–107, 2020.

[198] Jiangyi Li, Teng Yang, Minhao Yang, Peter R. Kinget, and Mingoo Seok. An area-efficient microprocessor-based SoC with an instruction-cache transformable to an ambient temperature sensor and a physically unclonable function. *IEEE Journal of Solid-State Circuits*, 53(3):728–737, 2018.

[199] Yuan Li, Paul Chow, Jiang Jiang, Minxuan Zhang, and Shaojun Wei. Software/hardware parallel long-period random number generation framework based on the well method. *IEEE Transactions on Very Large Scale Integration (VLSI) Systems*, 22(5):1054–1059, 2014.

[200] Zhen-Yu Liang, Hao-Hsuan Wei, and Tsung-Te Liu. A wide-range variation-resilient physically unclonable function in 28 nm. *IEEE Journal of Solid-State Circuits*, 55(3):817–825, 2020.

[201] Haohao Liao and Howard M. Heys. An integrated hardware platform for four different lightweight block ciphers. In *Proceedings of IEEE 28th Canadian Conference on Electrical and Computer Engineering (CCECE)*, Halifax, NS, Canada, May 2015.

[202] J. S. Liberty, A. Barrera, D. W. Boerstler, T. B. Chadwick, S. R. Cottier, H. P. Hofstee, J. A. Rosser, and M. L. Tsai. True hardware random number generation implemented in the 32-nm soi power7+ processor. *IBM Journal of Research and Development*, 57(6):1–7, 2013.

[203] D. Lim, J. W. Lee, B. Gassend, G. E. Suh, M. Van Dijk, and S. Devadas. Extracting secret keys from integrated circuits. *IEEE Transactions on Very Large Scale Integration (VLSI) Systems*, 13(10):1200–1205, 2005.

[204] Kuan Jen Lin, Shan Chien Fang, Shih Hsien Yang, and Cheng Chia Lo. Overcoming glitches and dissipation timing skews in design of DPA-resistant cryptographic hardware. In *Proceedings of Design, Automation & Test in Europe Conference & Exhibition*, Nice, France, April 2007.

[205] Chao Qun Liu, Yue Zheng, and Chip-Hong Chang. A new write-contention based dual-port SRAM PUF with multiple

response bits per cell. In *Proceedings of IEEE International Symposium on Circuits and Systems (ISCAS)*, Baltimore, MD, USA, May 2017.

[206] Dongsheng Liu, Cong Zhang, Hui Lin, Yuyang Chen, and Mingyu Zhang. A resource-efficient and side-channel secure hardware implementation of ring-LWE cryptographic processor. *IEEE Transactions on Circuits and Systems I: Regular Papers*, 66(4):1474–1483, 2019.

[207] Juhua Liu, Wei Li, and Guoqiang Bai. An improved S-box of lightweight block cipher roadrunner for hardware optimization. In *Proceedings of China Semiconductor Technology International Conference (CSTIC)*, Shanghai, China, March 2018.

[208] Kunyang Liu, Yue Min, Xuan Yang, Hanfeng Sun, and Hirofumi Shinohara. A 373-f2 0.21%-native-BER EE SRAM physically unclonable function with 2-d power-gated bit cells and VSS bias-based dark-bit detection. *IEEE Journal of Solid-State Circuits*, 55(6):1719–1732, 2020.

[209] Weiqiang Liu, Lei Zhang, Zhengran Zhang, Chongyan Gu, Chenghua Wang, Maire O'neill, and Fabrizio Lombardi. XOR-based low-cost reconfigurable PUFs for IoT security. *ACM Transactions on Embedded Computing Systems (TECS) - Special Issue on Cryptographic Engineering for IoT: Security Foundations, Lightweight Solutions, and Attacks and Regular*, 18(3):25:1–25:21, 2019.

[210] Yu Liu, Yier Jin, Aria Nosratinia, and Yiorgos Makris. Silicon demonstration of hardware trojan design and detection in wireless cryptographic ICs. *IEEE Transactions on Very Large Scale Integration (VLSI) Systems*, 25(4):1506–1519, 2017.

[211] Yu Liu, Georgios Volanis, Ke Huang, and Yiorgos Makris. Concurrent hardware trojan detection in wireless cryptographic ICs. In *Proceedings of IEEE International Test Conference (ITC)*, Anaheim, CA, USA, October 2015.

[212] Zhe Liu, Johann Großschädl, Zhi Hu, Kimmo Järvinen, Husen Wang, and Ingrid Verbauwhede. Elliptic curve cryptography with efficiently computable endomorphisms and its

hardware implementations for the internet of things. *IEEE Transactions on Computers*, 66(5):773–785, 2017.

[213] Zilong Liu, Dongsheng Liu, and Xuecheng Zou. An efficient and flexible hardware implementation of the dual-field elliptic curve cryptographic processor. *IEEE Transactions on Industrial Electronics*, 64(3):2353–2362, 2017.

[214] Xuyang Lu, Lingyu Hong, and Kaushik Sengupta. CMOS optical PUFs using noise-immune process-sensitive photonic crystals incorporating passive variations for robustness. *IEEE Journal of Solid-State Circuits*, 53(9):2709–2721, 2018.

[215] Rubén Lumbiarres-López, Mariano López-García, and Enrique Cantó-Navarro. Hardware architecture implemented on FPGA for protecting cryptographic keys against side-channel attacks. *IEEE Transactions on Dependable and Secure Computing*, 15(5):898–905, 2018.

[216] J. Lutz and A. Hasan. High performance FPGA based elliptic curve cryptographic co-processor. In *Proceedings of International Conference on Information Technology: Coding and Computing*, Las Vegas, NV, USA, April 2004.

[217] Michael X. Lyons and Kris Gaj. Sampling from discrete distributions in combinational hardware with application to post-quantum cryptography. In *Proceedings of Design, Automation & Test in Europe Conference & Exhibition (DATE)*, Grenoble, France, March 2020.

[218] Roel Maes. *Physically Unclonable Functions: Constructions, Properties and Applications.* Springer, 2013.

[219] Roel Maes, Pim Tuyls, and Ingrid Verbauwhede. A soft decision helper data algorithm for SRAM PUFs. In *Proceedings of IEEE International Symposium on Information Theory*, Seoul, South Korea, June-July 2009.

[220] Roel Maes and Ingrid Verbauwhede. Physically unclonable functions: A study on the state of the art and future research directions. In *Towards hardware-intrinsic security: Foundations and practice*, pages 3–37. Springer Nature, Switzerland, 2010.

[221] Mohammad Reza Mahmoodi, Zahra Fahimi, Shabnam Larimian, Hussein Nili, Hyugin Kim, and Dmitri B. Strukov. A strong physically unclonable function with ¿28° CRPs and ¡1.4% BER using passive reram technology. *IEEE Solid-State Circuits Letters*, 3(1):182–185, 2020.

[222] Svetlin A. Manavski. CUDA compatible GPU as an efficient hardware accelerator for AES cryptography. In *Proceedings of IEEE International Conference on Signal Processing and Communications*, Dubai, United Arab Emirates, November 2007.

[223] G.E. Mang and I. Mang. Properties of the RC6 cipher for a BIST hardware implementation. In *Proceedings of Military Communications Conference*, Anaheim, CA, USA, October 2002.

[224] I. Mang and G.E. Mang. Hardware implementation with off-line test capabilities of the RC6 block cipher. In *Proceedings of Military Communications Conference*, Anaheim, CA, USA, October 2002.

[225] Shohreh Sharif Mansouri and Elena Dubrova. An improved hardware implementation of the grain stream cipher. In *Proceedings of 13th Euromicro Conference on Digital System Design: Architectures, Methods and Tools*, Lille, France, September 2010.

[226] Farah Maqsood, Omar Farooq, and Wasim Ahmad. LFSR and PLA based complex code generator for stream cipher. In *Proceedings of International Multimedia, Signal Processing and Communication Technologies*, Aligarh, India, March 2009.

[227] I.L. Markov and D. Maslov. Uniformly-switching logic for cryptographic hardware. In *Proceedings of Design, Automation and Test in Europe*, Munich, Germany, March 2005.

[228] Takao Marukame, Tetsufumi Tanamoto, and Yuichiro Mitani. Extracting physically unclonable function from spin transfer switching characteristics in magnetic tunnel junctions. *IEEE Transactions on Magnetics*, 50(11):1–4, 2014.

[229] J. Mathew, S. Banerjee, H. Rahaman, D.K. Pradhan, S.P. Mohanty, and A.M. Jabir. On the synthesis of attack

tolerant cryptographic hardware. In *Proceedings of 18th IEEE/IFIP International Conference on VLSI and System-on-Chip*, Madrid, Spain, September 2010.

[230] Heath McCabe, Scott M. Koziol, Gregory L. Snider, and Enrique P. Blair. Tunable, hardware-based quantum random number generation using coupled quantum dots. *IEEE Transactions on Nanotechnology*, 19(1):292–296, 2020.

[231] Thomas McGrath, Ibrahim E. Bagci, Zhiming M. Wang, and Utz Roedigand Robert J. Young. A PUF taxonomy. *Applied Physics Reviews*, 6(1):1–26, 2019.

[232] C.J. Mcivor, M. Mcloone, and J.V. Mccanny. Hardware elliptic curve cryptographic processor over GF(p). *IEEE Transactions on Circuits and Systems I: Regular Papers*, 53(9):1946–1957, 2006.

[233] Saro Meguerdichian and Miodrag Potkonjak. Device aging-based physically unclonable functions. In *Proceedings of 48th ACM/EDAC/IEEE Design Automation Conference (DAC)*, New York, NY, USA, June 2011.

[234] Mohamadali Mehrabi, Christophe Doche, and Alireza Jolfaei. Elliptic curve cryptography point multiplication core for hardware security module. *IEEE Transactions on Computers (Early Access Article)*, pages 1–1, 2020.

[235] Ahmet Can Mert, Emre Karabulut, Erdinç Öztürk, Erkay Savas, Michela Becchi, and Aydin Aysu. A flexible and scalable NTT hardware: Applications from homomorphically encrypted deep learning to post-quantum cryptography. In *Proceedings of Design, Automation & Test in Europe Conference & Exhibition (DATE)*, Grenoble, France, March 2020.

[236] Hassen Mestiri, Fatma Kahri, Belgacem Bouallegue, and Mohsen Machhout. A CPA attack against cryptographic hardware implementation on SASEBO-GII. In *Proceedings of International Conference on Green Energy Conversion Systems (GECS)*, Hammamet, Tunisia, March 2017.

[237] H. Michail and C. Goutis. Holistic methodology for designing ultra high-speed SHA-1 hashing cryptographic module in hardware. In *Proceedings of IEEE International Conference*

on Electron Devices and Solid-State Circuits, Hong Kong, China, December 2008.

[238] Vincent Migliore, Maria Méndez Real, Vianney Lapotre, Arnaud Tisserand, Caroline Fontaine, and Guy Gogniat. Fast polynomial arithmetic for somewhat homomorphic encryption operations in hardware with Karatsuba algorithm. In *Proceedings of International Conference on Field-Programmable Technology (FPT)*, Xi'an, China, December 2016.

[239] Vincent Migliore, Maria Méndez Real, Vianney Lapotre, Arnaud Tisserand, Caroline Fontaine, and Guy Gogniat. Hardware/software co-design of an accelerator for FV homomorphic encryption scheme using Karatsuba algorithm. *IEEE Transactions on Computers*, 67(3):335–347, 2018.

[240] Aaron Mills. Design and evaluation of a delay-based FPGA physically unclonable function. Master's thesis, Iowa State University, Ames, Iowa, USA, 2012.

[241] Fan Mingyu, Wang Jinahua, and Wang Guangwei. A design of hardware cryptographic co-processor. In *Proceedings of IEEE Systems, Man and Cybernetics Society Information Assurance Workshop*, West Point, NY, USA, June 2003.

[242] Y. Mitsuyama, Z. Andales, T. Onoye, and I. Shirakawa. VLSI architecture of dynamically reconfigurable hardware-based cipher. In *Proceedings of IEEE International Symposium on Circuits and Systems*, Sydney, NSW, Australia, May 2001.

[243] Noriyuki Miura, Masanori Takahashi, Kazuki Nagatomo, and Makoto Nagata. Chaos, deterministic non-periodic flow, for chip-package-board interactive PUF. In *Proceedings of IEEE Asian Solid-State Circuits Conference (A-SSCC)*, Seoul, South Korea, November 2017.

[244] Iman Zarei Moghadam, Ali Shokouhi Rostami, and Mohammad Rasoul Tanhatalab. Designing a random number generator with novel parallel LFSR substructure for key stream ciphers. In *Proceedings of International Conference on Computer Design and Applications*, Qinhuangdao, China, June 2010.

[245] Sourav Mukherjee and Bibhudatta Sahoo. A survey on hardware implementation of idea cryptosystem. *Information Security Journal: A Global Perspective*, 20(4):210–218, 2011.

[246] Debdeep Mukhopadhyay and Rajat Subhra Chakraborty. Testability of cryptographic hardware and detection of hardware trojans. In *Proceedings of Asian Test Symposium*, New Delhi, India, November 2011.

[247] Caterina Munoz, Francisco Montoto, Francisco Cifuentes, and Javier Bustos-Jiménez. Building a threshold cryptographic distributed HSM with docker containers. In *Proceedings of CHILEAN Conference on Electrical, Electronics Engineering, Information and Communication Technologies (CHILECON)*, Pucon, Chile, October 2017.

[248] B. MuthuKumar and S. Jeevananthan. High speed hardware implementation of an elliptic curve cryptography (ECC) coprocessor. In *Proceedings of Trendz in Information Sciences & Computing (TISC2010)*, Chennai, India, December 2010.

[249] David Naccache and Patrice Frémanteau. Unforgeable identification device, identification device reader and method of identification, 1992. European Patent Office (EP0583709B1).

[250] Samad Najjar-Ghabel, Shamim Yousefi, and Mina Zolfy Lighvan. A high speed implementation counter mode cryptography using hardware parallelism. In *Proceedings of Eighth International Conference on Information and Knowledge Technology (IKT)*, Hamedan, Iran, September 2016.

[251] Longmei Nan, Zibin Dai, and Xuan Yang. Design of configurable LFSR instructions targeted at stream cipher processing. In *Proceedings of IEEE International Conference of Electron Devices and Solid-State Circuits*, Tianjin, China, November 2011.

[252] N. Nedjah, L.M. Mourelle, M. Santana, and S. Raposo. Massively parallel modular exponentiation method and its implementation in software and hardware for high-performance cryptographic systems. *IET Computers & Digital Techniques*, 6(5):290–301, 2012.

[253] Nadia Nedjah, Luiza de Macedo Mourelle, and Marco Paulo Cardoso. A compact piplined hardware implementation of

the AES-128 cipher. In *Proceedings of Third International Conference on Information Technology: New Generations*, Las Vegas, NV, USA, April 2006.

[254] Hamid Nejatollahi, Nikil Dutt, Sandip Ray, Francesco Regazzoni, Indranil Banerjee, and Rosario Cammarota. Software and hardware implementation of lattice-based cryptography schemes. Technical report, University of California, Irvine, November 2017.

[255] Ali Nemati, Soheil Feizi, Arash Ahmadi, Saeed Haghiri, Majid Ahmadi, and Shahpour Alirezaee. An efficient hardware implementation of few lightweight block cipher. In *Proceedings of the International Symposium on Artificial Intelligence and Signal Processing (AISP)*, Mashhad, Iran, March 2015.

[256] Duc Tri Nguyen, Viet B. Dang, and Kris Gaj. A high-level synthesis approach to the software/hardware codesign of NTT-based post-quantum cryptography algorithms. In *Proceedings of International Conference on Field-Programmable Technology (ICFPT)*, Tianjin, China, December 2019.

[257] Ha-Phuong Nguyen, The-Nghia Nguyen, Yeong-Seok Seo, Dosam Hwang, and Donghwa Shin. Correction of bit-aliasing in memristor-based physically unclonable functions with timing variability. *IEEE Access*, 7, 2019.

[258] Phuong Ha Nguyen and Durga Prasad Sahoo. Lightweight and secure PUFs: A survey. In *Proceedings of International Conference on Security, Privacy, and Applied Cryptography Engineering (SPACE)*, Pune, India, October 2014.

[259] P.K. Nasarathul Nisha, P.P. Deepthi, and K.S. Lalmohan. Design and analysis of stream cipher of low hardware complexity. In *Proceedings of International Conference on Communication Systems and Network Technologies*, Rajkot, India, May 2012.

[260] Kohei Nohara, Yusuke Nozaki, and Masaya Yoshikawa. Hardware trojan for ultra lightweight block cipher Piccolo. In *Proceedings of IEEE 4th Global Conference on Consumer Electronics (GCCE)*, Osaka, Japan, October 2015.

[261] Abdullah Al Noman, Roslina b. Mohd. Sidek, Abdul Rahman b. Ramli, and Liakot Ali. RC4A stream cipher for WLAN

security: A hardware approach. In *Proceedings of International Conference on Electrical and Computer Engineering*, Dhaka, Bangladesh, December 2008.

[262] J.M. Noras. Ciphering hardware for high-speed digital networks: a redoc iii implementation. *Electronics Letters*, 31(11):851–852, 1995.

[263] Yusuke Nozaki, Yoshiya Ikezaki, and Masaya Yoshikawa. Evaluation of PLFSR PUF with several implementation methods for FPGA. In *Proceedings of IEEE International Meeting for Future of Electron Devices, Kansai (IMFEDK)*, Kyoto, Japan, June 2017.

[264] Tobias Oder, Tim Güneysu, Felipe Valencia, Ayesha Khalid, Maire O'Neill, and Francesco Regazzoni. Lattice-based cryptography: From reconfigurable hardware to ASIC. In *Proceedings of International Symposium on Integrated Circuits (ISIC)*, Singapore, Singapore, December 2016.

[265] Takeshi Onomi and Yoshinao Mizugaki. Hardware random number generator using Josephson oscillation and SFQ logic circuits. *IEEE Transactions on Applied Superconductivity*, 30(7):1–5, 2020.

[266] R. Ostrovsky, A. Scafuro, I. Visconti, and A. Wadia. Universally composable secure computation with (malicious) physically uncloneable functions. In *Proceedings of Annual International Conference on the Theory and Applications of Cryptographic Techniques*, May 2013.

[267] Sudhanya P. and P. Muthu Krishnammal. Study of different silicon physical unclonable functions. In *Proceedings of International Conference on Wireless Communications, Signal Processing and Networking (WiSPNET)*, Chennai, India, March 2016.

[268] Jai Gopal Pandey, Tarun Goel, and Abhijit Karmakar. Hardware architectures for present block cipher and their FPGA implementations. *IET Circuits, Devices & Systems*, 13(7):410–420, 2019.

[269] A.P. Paplinski and N. Bhattacharjee. Hardware implementation of the Lehmer random number generator. *IEE*

Proceedings-Computers and Digital Techniques, 143(1):93–95, 1996.

[270] R. S. Pappu. *Physical one-way functions*. PhD thesis, Massachusetts Institute of Technology, 2001.

[271] R. S. Pappu, B. Recht, J. Taylor, and N. Gershenfeld. Physical one-way functions. *Science*, 297(5589):2026–30, 2002.

[272] L. Parrilla, A. Lloris, E. Castillo, and A. García. Minimum-clock-cycle Itoh-Tsujii algorithm hardware implementation for cryptography applications over $GF(2^m)$ fields. *Electronics Letters*, 48(18):1126–1128, 2012.

[273] Diogo Parrinha and Ricardo Chaves. Flexible and low-cost HSM based on non-volatile FPGAs. In *Proceedings of International Conference on ReConFigurable Computing and FPGAs (ReConFig)*, Cancun, Mexico, December 2017.

[274] Peter Pecho, Jan Nagy, and Petr Hanácek. Power consumption of hardware cryptography platform for wireless sensor. In *Proceedings of International Conference on Parallel and Distributed Computing, Applications and Technologies*, Higashi Hiroshima, Japan, December 2009.

[275] J. Perry, R. Schafer, and L. Rabiner. A digital hardware realization of a random number generator. *IEEE Transactions on Audio and Electroacoustics*, 20(4):236–240, 1972.

[276] Johannes Pfau, Maximilian Reuter, Tanja Harbaum, Klaus Hofmann, and Jürgen Becker. A hardware perspective on the ChaCha ciphers: Scalable ChaCha8/12/20 implementations ranging from 476 slices to bitrates of 175 Gbit/s. In *Proceedings of 32nd IEEE International System-on-Chip Conference (SOCC)*, Singapore, Singapore, September 2019.

[277] François Philipp, Conrad Klytta, Manfred Glesner, and Élvio Dutra. Hardware acceleration of combined cipher and forward error correction for low-power wireless applications. In *Proceedings of International Workshop on Reconfigurable and Communication-Centric Systems-on-Chip (ReCoSoC)*, York, UK, July 2012.

[278] Rainer Plaga and Dominik Merli. A new definition and classification of physical unclonable functions. *ArXiv*, abs/1501.06363, 2015.

[279] Ilia Polian and Martin Kreuzer. Fault-based attacks on cryptographic hardware. In *Proceedings of IEEE 16th International Symposium on Design and Diagnostics of Electronic Circuits & Systems (DDECS)*, Karlovy Vary, Czech Republic, April 2013.

[280] Jan Pospiil and Martin Novotný. Evaluating cryptanalytical strength of lightweight cipher present on reconfigurable hardware. In *Proceedings of 15th Euromicro Conference on Digital System Design*, Izmir, Turkey, September 2012.

[281] Timothy Potteiger and William H. Robinson. A one Zener diode, one memristor crossbar architecture for a write-time-based PUF. In *Proceedings of IEEE 58th International Midwest Symposium on Circuits and Systems (MWSCAS)*, Fort Collins, CO, USA, August 2015.

[282] Bikash Poudel, Sushil J. Louis, and Arslan Munir. Evolving side-channel resistant reconfigurable hardware for elliptic curve cryptography. In *Proceedings of IEEE Congress on Evolutionary Computation (CEC)*, San Sebastian, Spain, June 2017.

[283] Zhaoxing Qin, Michihiro Shintani, Kazunori Kuribara, Yasuhiro Ogasahara, and Takashi Sato. An experimental design of robust current-mode arbiter PUF using organic thin film transistors. In *Proceedings of 14th IEEE International Conference on Solid-State and Integrated Circuit Technology (ICSICT)*, Qingdao, China, October-November 2018.

[284] Md Shahed Enamul Quadir and John A. Chandy. Embedded systems authentication and encryption using strong PUF modeling. In *Proceedings of IEEE International Conference on Consumer Electronics (ICCE)*, Las Vegas, NV, USA, January 2020.

[285] Mahmood Azhar Qureshi and Arslan Munir. PUF-IPA: A PUF-based identity preserving protocol for internet of things authentication. In *Proceedings of IEEE 17th Annual Consumer Communications & Networking Conference (CCNC)*, Las Vegas, NV, USA, January 2020.

[286] Hanan Rady, Hagar Hossam, M.Sameh Saied, and Hassan Mostafa. Memristor-based AES key generation for low power

IoT hardware security modules. In *Proceedings of IEEE 62nd International Midwest Symposium on Circuits and Systems (MWSCAS)*, Dallas, TX, USA, August 2019.

[287] Mostafizur Rahman, Iqbalur Rahman Rokon, and Miftahur Rahman. Efficient hardware implementation of RSA cryptography. In *Proceedings of 3rd International Conference on Anti-counterfeiting, Security, and Identification in Communication*, Hong Kong, China, August 2009.

[288] Vikash Kumar Rai, Somanath Tripathy, and Jimson Mathew. 2SPUF: Machine learning attack resistant SRAM PUF. In *Proceedings of Third ISEA Conference on Security and Privacy (ISEA-ISAP)*, Guwahati, India, March 2020.

[289] Bahram Rashidi. Efficient and flexible hardware structures of the 128 bit CLEFIA block cipher. *IET Computers & Digital Techniques*, 14(2):69–79, 2020.

[290] Y. Ravishankar. *PUFs – An Extensive Survey*. PhD thesis, George Mason University, 2015.

[291] Trey Reece and William H. Robinson. Analysis of data-leak hardware trojans in AES cryptographic circuits. In *Proceedings of IEEE International Conference on Technologies for Homeland Security (HST)*, Waltham, MA, USA, November 2013.

[292] Jonathan Roberts. *Using Imperfect Semiconductor Systems for Unique Identification*. Springer, 2017.

[293] Gabriel Arquelau Pimenta Rodrigues, Robson De Oliveira Albuquerque, Gabriel De Oliveira Alves, Fábio Lúcio Lopes De Mendonça, William Ferreira Giozza, Rafael Timóteo De Sousa, and Ana Lucila Sandoval Orozco. Securing instant messages with hardware-based cryptography and authentication in browser extension. *IEEE Access*, 8:95137–95152, 2020.

[294] A. Romeo and M. Mattavelli. A hardware oriented analysis of cryptographic systems for multimedia applications. In *Proceedings of 10th European Signal Processing Conference*, Tampere, Finland, September 2000.

[295] Kurt Rosenfeld, Gavas Efstratios, and Ramesh Karri. Sensor physical unclonable functions. In *Proceedings of EEE International Symposium on Hardware-Oriented Security and Trust (HOST)*, 2010.

[296] T. Rossler, H. Leitold, and R. Posch. E-voting: a scalable approach using xml and hardware security modules. In *Proceedings of IEEE International Conference on e-Technology, e-Commerce and e-Service*, Hong Kong, China, March 2005.

[297] Vladimir Rožic and Ingrid Verbauwhede. Hardware-efficient post-processing architectures for true random number generators. *IEEE Transactions on Circuits and Systems II: Express Briefs*, 66(7):1242–1246, 2019.

[298] U. Rührmair. Oblivious transfer based on physical unclonable functions. In *Proceedings of International Conference on Trust and Trustworthy Computing*, June 2010.

[299] U. Rührmair, J.L. Martinez-Hurtado, X. Xu, C. Kraeh, C. Hilgers, D. Kononchuk, and W.P. Burleson. In *Proceedings of EEE Symposium on Security and Privacy*, 2015.

[300] U. Rührmair, F. Sehnke, J. Sölter, G. Dror, S. Devadas, and J. Schmidhuber. Modeling attacks on physical unclonable functions. In *Proceedings of the 17th ACM Conference on Computer and Communications Security*, October 2010.

[301] U. Rührmair and M. van Dijk. On the practical use of physical unclonable functions in oblivious transfer and bit commitment protocols. *Journal of Cryptographic Engineering*, 3(1):17–28, 2013.

[302] Ulrich Rührmair. Simpl systems: On a public key variant of physical unclonable functions. *IACR Cryptology ePrint Archive*, 2009(255), 2009.

[303] Ulrich Rührmair, Srinivas Devadas, and Farinaz Koushanfar. Security based on physical unclonability and disorder. In *Introduction to Hardware Security and Trust*, pages 65–102. Springer, New York, NY, 2012.

[304] Ulrich Rührmair and Daniel E. Holcomb. Pufs at a glance. In *Proceedings of Design, Automation & Test in Europe Conference & Exhibition (DATE)*, Dresden, Germany, March 2014.

[305] Ulrich Rührmair and Jan Sölter. Puf modeling attacks: An introduction and overview. In *Proceedings of Design, Automation & Test in Europe Conference & Exhibition (DATE)*, Dresden, Germany, March 2014.

[306] Shubham Sahay and Manan Suri. Recent trends in hardware security exploiting hybrid CMOS-resistive memory circuits. *Semiconductor Science and Technology*, 32(12), 2017.

[307] Shruti Sakhare and Dipti Sakhare. A review—hardware security using PUF (physical unclonable function). In *Proceedings of 2nd International Conference on Communications and Cyber Physical Engineering*, Hyderabad, Telangana, India, January 2019.

[308] Kazuo Sakiyama, Yu Sasaki, and Yang Li. Hardware implementations for block ciphers. In *Security of Block Ciphers: From Algorithm Design to Hardware Implementation*, pages 49–68. Wiley-IEEE Press, 2015.

[309] Ahmad Salman, William Diehl, and Jens-Peter Kaps. A light-weight hardware/software co-design for pairing-based cryptography with low power and energy consumption. In *Proceedings of International Conference on Field Programmable Technology (ICFPT)*, Melbourne, VIC, Australia, December 2017.

[310] Nagham Samir, Yousef Gamal, Ahmed N. El-Zeiny, Omar Mahmoud, Ahmed Shawky, AbdelRahman Saeed, and Hassan Mostafa. Energy-adaptive lightweight hardware security module using partial dynamic reconfiguration for energy limited internet of things applications. In *Proceedings of IEEE International Symposium on Circuits and Systems (ISCAS)*, Sapporo, Japan, May 2019.

[311] Ismail San and Nuray At. Compact hardware architecture for hummingbird cryptographic algorithm. In *Proceedings of 21st International Conference on Field Programmable Logic and Applications*, Chania, Greece, September 2011.

[312] M.M. Sandoval and C. Feregrino-Uribe. A hardware architecture for elliptic curve cryptography and lossless data compression. In *Proceedings of International Conference on Electronics, Communications and Computers*, Puebla, Mexico, March 2005.

[313] G. Saranya and S. Shanthi Rekha. Hardware implementation of a modified randomized cryptographic algorithm. In *Proceedings of International Conference on Advances in Engineering, Science And Management*, Nagapattinam, Tamil Nadu, India, March 2012.

[314] Pascal Sasdrich and Tim Géneysu. Cryptography for next generation TLS: Implementing the RFC 7748 elliptic Curve448 cryptosystem in hardware. In *Proceedings of 54th ACM/EDAC/IEEE Design Automation Conference (DAC)*, Austin, TX, USA, June 2017.

[315] Sudhir K. Satpathy, Sanu K. Mathew, Raghavan Kumar, Vikram Suresh, Mark A. Anders, Himanshu Kaul, Amit Agarwal, Steven Hsu, Ram K. Krishnamurthy, and Vivek De. An all-digital unified physically unclonable function and true random number generator featuring self-calibrating hierarchical Von Neumann extraction in 14-nm tri-gate CMOS. *IEEE Journal of Solid-State Circuits*, 54(4):1074–1085, 2019.

[316] André Schaller, Wenjie Xiong, Nikolaos Athanasios Anagnostopoulos, Muhammad Umair Saleem, Sebastian Gabmeyer, Boris Škoric, Stefan Katzenbeisser, and Jakub Szefer. Decay-based DRAM PUFs in commodity devices. *IEEE Transactions on Dependable and Secure Computing*, 16(3):462–475, 2019.

[317] Alexander Schaub, Jean-Luc Danger, Sylvain Guilley, and Olivier Rioul. An improved analysis of reliability and entropy for delay PUFs. In *Proceedings of 21st Euromicro Conference on Digital System Design (DSD)*, Prague, Czech Republic, August 2018.

[318] G. Selimis, P. Kitsos, and O. Koufopavlou. High performance cryptographic engine PANAMA: hardware implementation. In *Proceedings of 11th IEEE International Conference on Electronics, Circuits and Systems*, Tel Aviv, Israel, December 2004.

[319] Anirban Sengupta and Mahendra Rathor. Security of functionally obfuscated DSP core against removal attack using SHA-512 based key encryption hardware. *IEEE Access*, 7:4598–4610, 2019.

[320] Young-Ho Seo, Jong-Hyeon Kim, and Dong-Wook Kim. Hardware implementation of 128-bit symmetric cipher SEED. In *Proceedings of Second IEEE Asia Pacific Conference on ASICs*, Cheju, South Korea, August 2000.

[321] Jinho Seol, Seongwook Jin, Daewoo Lee, Jaehyuk Huh, and Seungryoul Maeng. A trusted IaaS environment with hardware security module. *IEEE Transactions on Services Computing*, 9(3):343–356, 2016.

[322] Mohammed Ali Shaik. Protecting agents from malicious hosts using trusted platform modules (TPM). In *Proceedings of Second International Conference on Inventive Communication and Computational Technologies (ICICCT)*, Coimbatore, India, April 2018.

[323] Alireza Shamsoshoara, Ashwija Reddy Korenda, Fatemeh Afghah, and Sherali Zeadally. A survey on hardware-based security mechanisms for internet of things. *ArXiv*, abs/1907.12525, 2019.

[324] M. Sharaf, H.A.K. Mansour, H.H. Zayed, and M.L. Shore. A complex linear feedback shift register design for the a5 keystream generator. In *Proceedings of the Twenty-Second National Radio Science Conference*, Cairo, Egypt, March 2005.

[325] Shantanu Sharma, Anton Burtsev, and Sharad Mehrotra. Advances in cryptography and secure hardware for data outsourcing. In *Proceedings of IEEE 36th International Conference on Data Engineering (ICDE)*, Dallas, TX, USA, April 2020.

[326] Vikrant Shende and Meghana Kulkarni. FPGA based hardware implementation of hybrid cryptographic algorithm for encryption and decryption. In *Proceedings of International Conference on Electrical, Electronics, Communication, Computer, and Optimization Techniques (ICEECCOT)*, Mysuru, India, December 2017.

[327] Abdulhadi Shoufan. A hardware security module for quadrotor communication. In *Proceedings of International Conference on Field-Programmable Technology*, Seoul, South Korea, December 2012.

[328] G. Simmons. A system for verifying user identity and authorization at the point-of sale or access. *Cryptologia*, 8(1):1–21, 1984.

[329] G. Simmons. Identification of data, devices, documents and individuals. In *Proceedings of IEEE International Carnahan Conference on Security Technology*, Taipei, Taiwan, October 1991.

[330] Arvind Singh, Nikhil Chawla, Monodeep Kar, and Saibal Mukhopadhyay. Energy efficient and side-channel secure hardware architecture for lightweight cipher SIMON. In *Proceedings of IEEE International Symposium on Hardware Oriented Security and Trust (HOST)*, Washington, DC, USA, April 2018.

[331] Arvind Singh, Nikhil Chawla, Jong Hwan Ko, Monodeep Kar, and Saibal Mukhopadhyay. Energy efficient and side-channel secure cryptographic hardware for IoT-edge nodes. *IEEE Internet of Things Journal*, 6(1):421–434, 2019.

[332] Prasoon Lata Singh, Alak Majumder, Barnali Chowdhury, Ranvijay Singh, and Nikhil Mishra. A novel realization of reversible LFSR for its application in cryptography. In *Proceedings of 2nd International Conference on Signal Processing and Integrated Networks (SPIN)*, Noida, India, February 2015.

[333] Nicolas Sklavos. Cryptographic hardware & embedded systems for communications. In *Proceedings of IEEE First AESS European Conference on Satellite Telecommunications (ESTEL)*, Rome, Italy, October 2012.

[334] Nicolas Sklavos. Towards to SHA-3 hashing standard for secure communications: On the hardware evaluation development. *IEEE Latin America Transactions*, 10(1):1433–1434, 2012.

[335] Amos Matthew Smith and H. Shelton Jacinto. Reconfigurable integrated optical interferometer network-based physically unclonable function. *Journal of Lightwave Technology (Early Access Article)*, pages 1–1, 2020.

[336] Srivatsan Subramanian, Mehran Mozaffari-Kermani, Reza Azarderakhsh, and Mehrdad Nojoumian. Reliable hardware architectures for cryptographic block ciphers LED and

HIGHT. *IEEE Transactions on Computer-Aided Design of Integrated Circuits and Systems*, 36(10):1750–1758, 2017.

[337] Manan Suri and Supriya Chakraborty. High-quality PUF extraction from commercial RRAM using switching-time variability. In *Proceedings of International Memory Workshop (IMW)*, Kyoto, Japan, May 2018.

[338] Soubhagya Sutar, Arnab Raha, and Vijay Raghunathan. D-PUF: An intrinsically reconfigurable DRAM PUF for device authentication in embedded systems. In *Proceedings of International Conference on Compliers, Architectures, and Synthesis of Embedded Systems (CASES)*, Pittsburgh, PA, USA, October 2016.

[339] Shahin Tajik. *On the Physical Security of Physically Unclonable Functions (T-Labs Series in Telecommunication Services)*. Springer, 2018.

[340] Hai Tao, Md Zakirul Alam Bhuiyan, Ahmed N. Abdalla, Mohammad Mehedi Hassan, Jasni Mohamad Zain, and Thaier Hayajneh. Secured data collection with hardware-based ciphers for IoT-based healthcare. *IEEE Internet of Things Journal*, 6(1):410–420, 2019.

[341] John Teifel. Asynchronous cryptographic hardware design. In *Proceedings of 40th Annual 2006 International Carnahan Conference on Security Technology*, Lexington, KY, USA, October 2006.

[342] A.F. Tenca and L.A. Tawalbeh. Algorithm for unified modular division in GF(p) and GF(2^n) suitable for cryptographic hardware. *Electronics Letters*, 40(5):304–306, 2004.

[343] Himanshu Thapliyal and Mark Zwolinski. Reversible logic to cryptographic hardware: A new paradigm. In *Proceedings of 49th IEEE International Midwest Symposium on Circuits and Systems*, San Juan, Puerto Rico, August 2006.

[344] A. Thiruneelakandan and T. Thirumurugan. An approach towards improved cyber security by hardware acceleration of OpenSSL cryptographic functions. In *Proceedings of International Conference on Electronics, Communication and Computing Technologies*, Pauls Nagar, India, September 2011.

[345] Victor Tomashevich, Yaara Neumeier, Raghavan Kumar, Osnat Keren, and Ilia Polian. Protecting cryptographic hardware against malicious attacks by nonlinear robust codes. In *Proceedings of IEEE International Symposium on Defect and Fault Tolerance in VLSI and Nanotechnology Systems (DFT)*, Amsterdam, Netherlands, October 2014.

[346] Cesar Torres-Huitzil. Hardware realization of a lightweight 2d cellular automata-based cipher for image encryption. In *Proceedings of IEEE 4th Latin American Symposium on Circuits and Systems (LASCAS)*, Cusco, Peru, March 2013.

[347] Shailendra Kumar Tripathi, K.K. Soundra Pandian, and Bhupendra Gupta. Hardware implementation of dynamic key value based stream cipher using chaotic logistic map. In *Proceedings of 2nd International Conference on Trends in Electronics and Informatics (ICOEI)*, Tirunelveli, India, May 2018.

[348] Shailendra Kumar Tripathi, K.K. Soundra Pandian, and Bhupendra Gupta. Hardware implementation of dynamic key value based stream cipher using chaotic logistic map. In *Proceedings of 2nd International Conference on Trends in Electronics and Informatics (ICOEI)*, Tirunelveli, India, May 2018.

[349] Joshua Trujillo, Christian Merino, and Payman Zarkesh-Ha. SRAM physically unclonable functions implemented on silicon germanium. In *Proceedings of IEEE International Symposium on Circuits and Systems (ISCAS)*, Sapporo, Japan, May 2019.

[350] Taner Tuncer and Erdinç Avaroglu. Random number generation with LFSR based stream cipher algorithms. In *Proceedings of 40th International Convention on Information and Communication Technology, Electronics and Microelectronics (MIPRO)*, Opatija, Croatia, May 2017.

[351] Pim Tuyls, Boris koric, and Tom Kevenaar. *Security with Noisy Data: On Private Biometrics, Secure Key Storage and Anti-Counterfeiting*. Springer, 2007.

[352] U. U. Rührmair, C. Jaeger, M. Bator, M. Stutzmann, P. Lugli, and G. Csaba. Applications of high-capacity cross-

bar memories in cryptography. *IEEE Transactions on Nanotechnology*, 10(3):489–498, 2010.

[353] Darshana Upadhyay, Trishla Shah, and Priyanka Sharma. Cryptanalysis of hardware based stream ciphers and implementation of GSM stream cipher to propose a novel approach for designing n-bit LFSR stream cipher. In *Proceedings of 19th International Symposium on VLSI Design and Test*, Ahmedabad, India, June 2015.

[354] Mohammad Usmani. Applications of physical unclonable functions on ASICs and applications of physical unclonable functions on ASICs and FPGAs. Master's thesis, University of, Amherst, Massachusetts, USA, 2018.

[355] P.C. van Oorschot, A. Somayaji, and G. Wurster. Hardware-assisted circumvention of self-hashing software tamper resistance. *IEEE Transactions on Dependable and Secure Computing*, 2(2):82–92, 2005.

[356] Aishwarya Bahudhanam Venkatasubramaniyan and Arindam Sanyal. Physically unclonable function based on voltage divider arrays in subthreshold region. In *Proceedings of IEEE 61st International Midwest Symposium on Circuits and Systems (MWSCAS)*, Windsor, ON, Canada, Canada, August 2018.

[357] Harsh Kumar Verma and Ravindra Kumar Singh. Linear feedback shift register based unique random number generator. *International Journal of Computer Science and Informatics*, 3(4):273–279, 2014.

[358] Satyanarayana Vollala, B. Shameedha Begum, Amit D. Joshi, and N. Ramasubramanian. High-radix modular exponentiation for hardware implementation of public-key cryptography. In *Proceedings of International Conference on Computing, Analytics and Security Trends (CAST)*, Pune, India, December 2016.

[359] Christian Wachsmann and Ahmad-Reza Sadegh. *Physically Unclonable Functions (PUFs): Applications, Models, and Future Directions*. Morgan & Claypool, San Rafael, CA 94901, USA, 1 edition, 2014.

[360] Christian Wachsmann and Ahmad-Reza Sadegh. *Physically Unclonable Functions (PUFs): Applications, Models, and Future Directions*. Morgan & Claypool, San Rafael, CA 94901, USA, 1 edition, 2014.

[361] Akshay Wali, Akhil Dodda, Yang Wu, Andrew Pannone, Likhith Kumar Reddy Usthili, Sahin Kaya Ozdemir, Ibrahim Tarik Ozbolat, and Saptarshi Das. Biological physically unclonable function. *Communications Physics*, 2:1–10, 2019.

[362] Chao Wang, Jun Zhou, Katti Guruprasad, Xin Liu, Roshan Weerasekera, and Tony T. Kim. TSV-based PUF circuit for 3DIC sensor nodes in IoT applications. In *Proceedings of International Conference on Electron Devices and Solid-State Circuits (EDSSC)*, Singapore, Singapore, June 2015.

[363] DeWei Wang, ZhenHui Zhang, LiJi Wu, and XiangMin Zhang. Hardware design of lightweight stream cipher PUF-FIN algorithm for anti-cooperation. In *Proceedings of 12th IEEE International Conference on Anti-counterfeiting, Security, and Identification (ASID)*, Xiamen, China, April 2018.

[364] Di Wang, Liji Wu, and Xiangmin Zhang. Key-leakage hardware trojan with super concealment based on the fault injection for block cipher of SM4. *Electronics Letters*, 54(13):810–812, 2018.

[365] Lih-Yang Wang, Chi-Sung Laih, Hang-Geng Tsai, and Nern-Min Huang. On the hardware design for DES cipher in tamper resistant devices against differential fault analysis. In *Proceedings of IEEE International Symposium on Circuits and Systems (ISCAS)*, Geneva, Switzerland, May 2000.

[366] Lih-Yang Wang, Chi-Sung Laih, Hang-Geng Tsai, and Nern-Min Huang. On the hardware design for DES cipher in tamper resistant devices against differential fault analysis. In *Proceedings of IEEE International Symposium on Circuits and Systems (ISCAS)*, Geneva, Switzerland, May 2000.

[367] Liwei Wang, Chunhua He, Bo Hou, and ShaoFeng Xie. Detection of information-leak hardware trojan in AES cryptographic circuits. In *Proceedings of 10th International Conference on Reliability, Maintainability and Safety (ICRMS)*, Guangzhou, China, August 2014.

[368] Yi Wang, J. Leiwo, and T. Srikanthan. Efficient high radix modular multiplication for high-speed computing in reconfigurable hardware [cryptographic applications]. In *Proceedings of IEEE International Symposium on Circuits and Systems*, Kobe, Japan, May 2005.

[369] Dai Watanabe, Kota Ideguchi, Jun Kitahara, Kenichiro Muto, Hiroki Furuichi, and Toshinobu Kaneko. Enocoro-80: A hardware oriented stream cipher. In *Proceedings of Third International Conference on Availability, Reliability and Security*, Barcelona, Spain, March 2008.

[370] Davy Wolfs, Kris Aerts, and Nele Mentens. Design space exploration for automatically generated cryptographic hardware using functional languages. In *Proceedings of International Conference on Field Programmable Logic and Applications (FPL)*, Oslo, Norway, August 2012.

[371] Chau-Wai Wong and Min Wu. Counterfeit detection using paper PUF and mobile cameras. In *Proceedings of IEEE International Workshop on Information Forensics and Security*, Rome, Italy, November 2015.

[372] Kan Xiao, Md. Tauhidur Rahman, Domenic Forte, Yu Huang, Mei Su, and Mohammad Tehranipoor. Bit selection algorithm suitable for high-volume production of SRAM-PUF. In *Proceedings of IEEE International Symposium on Hardware-Oriented Security and Trust (HOST)*, Arlington, VA, USA, May 2014.

[373] Hongfeng Xie, Huiyun Li, and Guoqing Xu. Hardware trojan prevention based on fully homomorphic encryption. In *Proceedings of IEEE International Conference on Information and Automation*, Lijiang, China, August 2015.

[374] Jiafeng Xie, Kanad Basu, Kris Gaj, and Ujjwal Guin. Special session: The recent advance in hardware implementation of post-quantum cryptography. In *Proceedings of IEEE 38th VLSI Test Symposium (VTS)*, San Diego, CA, USA, April 2020.

[375] Yuhang Xing, Min Li, and Litao Wang. Differences of stream cipher implementations based on LFSR multiplication circuits and division circuits. In *Proceedings of 6th Interna-*

tional Conference on Biomedical Engineering and Informatics, Hangzhou, China, February 2013.

[376] Wenjie Xiong, André Schaller, Stefan Katzenbeisser, and Jakub Szefer. Software protection using dynamic PUFs. *IEEE Transactions on Information Forensics and Security*, 15(1):2053–2068, 2020.

[377] Chengxi Xu, Ronggui Hu, Yongyi Wang, and Fan Shi. A noniterative reconstruction algorithm for LFSR PRNG. In *Proceedings of International Conference on Computer Science and Network Technology*, Changchun, China, December 2012.

[378] Junjie Yan and Howard M. Heys. Hardware implementation of the Salsa20 and Phelix stream ciphers. In *Proceedings of Canadian Conference on Electrical and Computer Engineering*, Vancouver, BC, Canada, April 2007.

[379] Jianguo Yang, Xing Li, Tao Wang, Xiaoyong Xue, Zhiliang Hong, Yuanyuan Wang, David Wei Zhang, and Hongliang Lu. A physically unclonable function with BER ¡ 0.35% for secure chip authentication using write speed variation of RRAM. In *Proceedings of European Solid-State Device Research Conference (ESSDERC)*, Dresden, Germany, September 2018.

[380] Kaiyuan Yang, Qing Dong, David Blaauw, and Dennis Sylvester. A 553f2 2-transistor amplifier-based physically unclonable function (PUF) with 1.67% native instability. In *Proceedings of IEEE International Solid-State Circuits Conference (ISSCC)*, San Francisco, CA, USA, February 2017.

[381] Teng Yang, Jiangyi Li, Minhao Yang, Peter R. Kinget, and Mingoo Seok. An area-efficient microcontroller with an instruction-cache transformable to an ambient temperature sensor and a physically unclonable function. In *Proceedings of IEEE Custom Integrated Circuits Conference (CICC)*, Austin, TX, USA, May 2017.

[382] Yasir, Ning Wu, Xiao Qiang Zhang, and Muhammad Rehan Yahya. Highly optimised reconfigurable hardware architecture of 64 bit block ciphers MISTY1 and KASUMI. *Electronics Letters*, 53(1):10–12, 2017.

[383] Jing Ye, Yue Gong, Yu Hu, and Xiaowei Li. Polymorphic PUF: Exploiting reconfigurability of CPU+FPGA SoC to resist modeling attack. In *Proceedings of Asian Hardware Oriented Security and Trust Symposium (AsianHOST)*, Beijing, China, October 2017.

[384] Chi-En Yin and Gang Qu. Improving PUF security with regression-based distiller. In *Proceedings of 50th ACM/EDAC/IEEE Design Automation Conference (DAC)*, Austin, TX, USA, May-June 2013.

[385] Ville Yli-Mäyry, Naofumi Homma, and Takafumi Aoki. Chosen-input side-channel analysis on unrolled light-weight cryptographic hardware. In *Proceedings of 18th International Symposium on Quality Electronic Design (ISQED)*, Santa Clara, CA, USA, March 2017.

[386] Weize Yu and Yiming Wen. Efficient hybrid side-channel/machine learning attack on XOR PUFs. *Electronics Letters*, 55(20):1080–1082, 2019.

[387] Wenqian Yu, Weigang Li, Junyuan Wang, and Changzheng Wei. A study of HSM based key protection in encryption file system. In *Proceedings of IEEE Conference on Communications and Network Security (CNS)*, Philadelphia, PA, USA, October 2016.

[388] Xiao Yu, Ning Wu, Fang Zhou, Jinbao Zhang, and Xinggan Zhang. A compact hardware implementation for the SCA-resistant present cipher. In *Proceedings of 45th Annual Conference of the IEEE Industrial Electronics Society*, Lisbon, Portugal, October 2019.

[389] Ji-Liang Zhang, Gang Qu, Yong-Qiang Lv, and Qiang Zhou. A survey on silicon PUFs and recent advances in ring oscillator PUFs. *Journal of Computer Science and Technology*, 29(4):664–678, 2014.

[390] Jiahong Zhang, Tinggang Xiong, and Xiangyan Fang. A fast hardware implementation of elliptic curve cryptography. In *Proceedings of First International Conference on Information Science and Engineering*, Nanjing, China, December 2009.

[391] Li Zhang, Chunhong Wang, Tao Pei, and Yong Zeng. Another analysis of a synchronizing stream cipher combining LFSR and FCSR. In *Proceedings of International Conference on Networking and Network Applications (NaNA)*, Daegu, Korea (South), October 2019.

[392] Kai Zhou, Huaguo Liang, Yue Jiang, Zhengfeng Huang, Cuiyun Jiang, and Yingchun Lu. FPGA-based RO PUF with low overhead and high stability. *Electronics Letters*, 55(9):510–513, 2019.

[393] Nusa Zidaric, Mark Aagaard, and Guang Gong. Hardware optimizations and analysis for the WG-16 cipher with tower field arithmetic. *IEEE Transactions on Computers*, 68(1):67–82, 2019.

Index

Note: *Italicized* and **bold** pages refer to figures and tables respectively.